Light Quick Breads

THE ADVOCATE COLLECTION

THE LOW-FAT KITCHEN

Light Quick Breads

Over 65 Recipes for Sweet and Savory Low-Fat Quick Breads and Spreads

SIGAL SEEBER

Clarkson Potter/Publishers
New York

Published by Clarkson N. Potter / Publishers, 201 East 50th Street, New York, New York 10022. Member of the Crown Publishing Group.

Random House, Inc. New York, Toronto, London, Sydney, Auckland

CLARKSON N. POTTER, POTTER, and colophon are trademarks of Clarkson N. Potter, Inc.

Printed in the United States of America

Design by Susan DeStaebler

Library of Congress Cataloging-in Publication Data
Seeber, Sigal.
    The low-fat kitchen : light quick breads : over 65 recipes for sweet and savory low-fat quick breads and spreads / Sigal Seeber.
    1. Bread. 2. Low-fat diet—Recipes. I. Title.
TX769.S3985   1996
641.8'15—dc20   94-4118

ISBN 0-517-70552-4

10   9   8   7   6   5   4   3   2   1

First Edition

Contents

Introduction   7

Breakfast and Brunch Breads   13

Snack Breads   29

Fat-Free Breads   45

Savory Breads   59

Dessert Breads   73

Spreads   87

Index   93

Conversion Chart   96

Introduction

When family or friends come into a home perfumed with the aroma of freshly baked bread, they know something special is in store. It doesn't necessarily mean a celebratory meal is being prepared, or that someone spent all day baking, either—creating a warm touch or personalizing a dinner with homemade bread can be as simple as serving a delicious quick bread.

Quick breads, leavened with baking powder or baking soda, are much faster to prepare than breads made with yeast. Quick breads also lend themselves to as much variety as traditional rising breads, and different flours or flavors can produce exciting results. Throughout our culinary history, American cooks have invented a unique bounty of quick breads that are varied, delicious, and now low in fat, too.

Traditionally, most quick-bread recipes featured what today is considered an unhealthy amount of fat, refined sugar, sodium, and calories. In the last few years, dietary health concerns have changed the way we cook and eat, and the latest studies on nutrition are front-page news. More studies show that eating well to reduce the risks of heart problems, cancer, and high cholesterol includes a regime that is not only high in fiber but low in fat. It is clear that we want to enjoy good health as much as we enjoy good food.

The breads are divided into chapters that describe the types of loaves in the section, or suggest times when these breads might be served. However, you should feel free to browse through the book and decide which bread seems best for your occasion; there is certainly no rule against enjoying a slice of Maple-Cranberry Corn Bread with afternoon tea!

Light Quick Breads offers recipes that combine great taste with good nutrition. Excess fat, sugar, and sodium are eliminated and replaced with fruit purees, spices, and herbs; plus you'll learn new techniques of extracting the most flavor from your ingredients. You'll find reinterpretations of traditional favorites that meet recommended nutritional guidelines—currently at 30 percent calories from fat per serving—and let you continue enjoying one of life's great pleasures, the fresh loaf of bread.

MEASURING

A set of calibrated measuring cups and spoons is essential for baking low-fat bread. The accurate measure of dry ingredients depends on how you have filled the cup. Always stir the flour to remove any clumps before you measure. Spoon the flour into the cup—don't press or tamp the flour down—and then run the flat edge of a knife or spatula across the top to remove the excess. For dry ingredients use a measuring cup designed for solids. Liquids should be measured in a clear glass or plastic cup with a spout.

MIXING

Low-fat quick breads require only slight gluten development, which ensures the desirable quality of tenderness.

Therefore the mixing method should be short and gentle. Batters are mixed as little as possible, only until the dry ingredients are moistened and not fully incorporated. The blended batter will look lumpy; do not attempt to achieve a smooth batter. The danger of overmixing is that the bread can become tough and chewy, meaning too much gluten has formed. For most breads contained in this book, ten to fifteen strokes should be sufficient.

BAKING AND PANS

Preheat the oven for at least fifteen to thirty minutes before baking the bread. Be sure the oven is calibrated properly; accurate oven temperature is very important for low-fat bread baking. If you have doubts about the accuracy of your oven setting, check the temperature with an oven thermometer. Low-fat breads need less baking time than breads with higher fat contents, and overbaking can cause the bread to become dry. Generally speaking, the breads should be baked in the middle or upper third of the oven. This will keep them away from the source of direct heat, and they will bake evenly. A good test for doneness is to insert a wooden skewer in the middle of a loaf. If it comes out clean, the bread is ready.

For most breads in this book, baking is done in a $9 \times 5 \times 2\frac{1}{2}$ inch loaf pan. Different pans can be used, including tubes, bundts, and all sizes of skillets and baking pans. In general, the more shallow the baking pan, the shorter the cooking time. Remember, all ingredients, oven temperatures, and baking pans are basic guidelines and are not carved in stone. Feel free to experiment and test your own ideas. You will find your knowledge and confidence will improve greatly as you move on your way to becoming a successful baker.

COOLING

Immediately after the bread is removed from the oven, it should remain in the pan on a cooling rack for about ten minutes until it has cooled slightly. During this time, it will also become firmer, and there will be less chance of the loaf breaking. Run a knife around the edge of the pan and carefully turn it upside down. The loaf should come out easily and in one piece. Let the bread cool further on a wire rack. This will allow steam to escape. If the bread sits for too long in the baking container, steam causes the bread to become soggy. Wait for at least forty-five minutes before slicing. The bread should be stored in a plastic bag or container at room temperature for the first two days to keep in moisture, and after that refrigerated, tightly covered, to prevent mold from forming.

FREEZING

Before you freeze any bread, it should be tightly wrapped in aluminum foil and then sealed in a plastic bag. Most quick breads will freeze well and keep for up to two months in the freezer. It will take two hours for a loaf to thaw at room temperature, overnight to defrost in the refrigerator, and thirty minutes in a warm oven. When thawing in the oven, remove only the plastic and place the bread in the oven still wrapped in the foil. The bread should be served soon after thawing. Breads can be sliced before freezing so that a few slices can be eaten at a time, but note that freezing in this fashion may reduce moisture content.

FAT SUBSTITUTES

If you need to decrease your cholesterol and fat, use two large egg whites in place of one whole large egg in a recipe. Additional fruit purees, grated zest, fresh herbs, and/or dried spices will increase the flavor, moisture, and tenderness without adding calories from fat. Liquid sweeteners such as pure maple syrup and honey also add flavor and moistness.

COOKING SPRAY

When you choose a nonstick cooking spray, it is usually a good idea to choose one with a neutral flavor. Those made with canola oil will impart the least amount of flavor to any bread you may be baking. Avoid olive oil–flavored sprays, which may have a stronger flavor that could interfere with the taste of the bread.

Breakfast and Brunch Breads

Sweet Apple Bread

Apple butter and sauce add moisture and concentrated flavor without adding extra fat. Slice thin, and layer with Strawberry Jam (see page 91).

1 cup all-purpose flour
2 teaspoons baking soda
2 teaspoons ground cinnamon
1 teaspoon salt
1 cup oat bran
2 large egg whites, lightly beaten

$\frac{1}{2}$ cup apple butter
$\frac{1}{2}$ cup pure maple syrup
$\frac{1}{2}$ cup applesauce
1 tablespoon canola oil or melted unsalted butter
1 large Granny Smith apple, peeled, cored, and cut into $\frac{1}{4}$-inch dice (about 1 cup)

Preheat the oven to 375° F. Lightly coat a 9 × 5 × 2½ inch loaf pan with nonstick cooking spray.

In a large bowl, sift together the flour, baking soda, cinnamon, and salt. Add the oat bran and stir to incorporate thoroughly. In a small bowl, whisk together the egg whites, apple butter, maple syrup, applesauce, and oil or butter until well mixed. Add three-fourths of the diced apple. Stir the liquid ingredients into the dry ingredients just until the dry are moistened, about 10 strokes.

Spoon the batter into the loaf pan and top with the remaining apple. Bake for 50 to 60 minutes, or until light golden brown and a wooden skewer inserted in the center of the loaf comes out clean.

Cool for 10 minutes in the pan. Remove from the pan and serve warm or transfer to a wire rack to cool completely.

MAKES 12 SLICES
Per slice: 132 cal. (11% from fat), 1.6 g. fat, 2.2 g. fiber

Whole Wheat—Banana Bread

Overripe bananas are the secret to this old-fashioned favorite. This is a healthy next-day snack, especially when topped with Apricot-Lemon Spread (see page 88).

1 cup whole wheat flour
$^3/_4$ cup all-purpose flour
$^1/_4$ cup wheat germ
$^1/_2$ cup light brown sugar
2 teaspoons baking powder
$^1/_2$ teaspoon baking soda
$^1/_4$ teaspoon salt
2 large eggs, lightly beaten
2 medium bananas, mashed

1 cup nonfat buttermilk
2 tablespoons unsalted
    butter, melted

Banana-Crunch Topping

1 medium banana, cut into
    $^1/_4$-inch slices
1 teaspoon light brown sugar
1 tablespoon wheat germ

Preheat the oven to 375° F. Lightly coat a 9 × 5 × 2½ inch loaf pan with nonstick cooking spray.

In a large mixing bowl, combine the flours, wheat germ, brown sugar, baking powder, baking soda, and salt. In a small mixing bowl, whisk together the eggs, bananas, buttermilk, and butter until well mixed. Stir the liquid ingredients into the dry ingredients just until the dry are moistened, about 10 strokes.

Spoon the batter into the loaf pan and arrange the banana slices on top. Sprinkle with the sugar and wheat germ. Bake for 40 to 50 minutes, or until golden brown and a wooden skewer inserted in the center of the loaf comes out clean.

Cool for 10 minutes in the baking pan. Remove from the pan and serve warm or transfer to a wire rack to cool completely.

MAKES 12 SLICES
Per slice: 161 cal. (20% from fat), 3.6 g. fat, 2.4 g. fiber

Apricot-Pecan Bread

Not just for special breakfasts, this bread is good to have on hand anytime. The apricots moisten the bread and add a natural sweetness. Serve it warm with fruit and nonfat yogurt or a scoop of low-fat cottage cheese.

1 cup dried apricots
½ cup golden raisins
1 cup water
2 cups all-purpose flour
½ cup light brown sugar
2 teaspoons baking powder
1 teaspoon baking soda
1 teaspoon salt
2 large eggs, lightly beaten
2 teaspoons grated lemon zest
2 tablespoons fresh lemon
   juice

2 tablespoons unsalted
   butter, melted
2 tablespoons chopped
   pecans

Apricot Glaze

2 tablespoons reserved
   apricot puree (see recipe
   procedure)
2 tablespoons fresh lemon
   juice

Preheat the oven to 375° F. Lightly coat a 9 × 5 × 2½ inch loaf pan with nonstick cooking spray.

Combine the apricots, the golden raisins, and the water in a medium saucepan. Bring to a boil over medium-high heat. Reduce the heat and simmer for 10 minutes, or until the fruits are plumped. Remove from the heat and let cool. Do not drain. Place in a blender or food processor and puree until smooth. Cool and reserve 2 tablespoons for the glaze.

In a large bowl sift together the flour, sugar, baking powder, baking soda, and salt. In a small bowl whisk together the eggs, lemon zest, lemon juice, butter, and apricot puree until well mixed. Stir the liquid ingredients into the dry ingredients just until the dry are moistened, about 10 strokes.

Spoon the batter into the loaf pan and sprinkle the chopped pecans on top. Bake for 50 to 60 minutes, or until light golden brown and a wooden skewer inserted in the center of the loaf comes out clean.

To make the glaze, while the bread is baking, combine the reserved 2 tablespoons of apricot puree with the lemon juice. When the bread is done, remove from oven and brush the top with the glaze, until all is used.

Cool for 10 minutes in the baking pan. Remove from the pan and serve warm, or transfer to a wire rack to cool completely.

MAKES 12 SLICES
Per slice: 176 cal. (18% from fat), 3.6 g. fat, 1.8 g. fiber

Blueberry-Spice Bread

This is delicious when made with fresh wild blueberries. If you do use frozen, add them to the batter unthawed.

2 cups all-purpose flour
4 tablespoons sugar
3 teaspoons baking powder
1/2 teaspoon salt
1/4 teaspoon ground nutmeg
1/4 teaspoon ground allspice
1/2 teaspoon ground cinnamon

2 teaspoons grated orange zest
1 1/2 cups fresh or frozen blueberries
2 large eggs, lightly beaten
1 cup skim milk
3 tablespoons unsalted butter, melted

Preheat the oven to 375° F. Lightly coat a 9 × 5 × 2 1/2 inch loaf pan with nonstick cooking spray.

In a large bowl, sift together the flour, 3 tablespoons of the sugar, the baking powder, salt, nutmeg, allspice, and 1/4 teaspoon of the cinnamon. Add the orange zest. Measure 1 tablespoon of the mixture in a small bowl and add the blueberries. Toss lightly until the blueberries are coated with the flour mixture, and set aside. (This helps to prevent the fruit from all settling to the bottom of the bread during baking.)

In a small bowl, whisk together the eggs, milk, and butter until well mixed. Stir the liquid ingredients into the dry ingredients just until the dry are moistened; use about 10 strokes. Gently fold in the blueberries.

Spoon the batter into the loaf pan and sprinkle the top of the bread with the remaining 1/4 teaspoon cinnamon and 1 tablespoon sugar. Bake for 50 to 60 minutes, or until light golden brown and a wooden skewer inserted in the center of the loaf comes out clean.

Cool for 10 minutes and remove from the baking pan. Serve warm or transfer to a wire rack.

MAKES 12 SLICES
Per slice: 142 cal. (25% from fat), 4.0 g. fat, 1.0 g. fiber

Whole Wheat–Molasses Bread

Hearty and filling, this bread is especially tasty when served warm and topped with yogurt and fresh fruit.

2 cups whole wheat flour	1½ cups nonfat plain yogurt
1 teaspoon baking soda	¾ cup molasses
2 teaspoons baking powder	3 tablespoons unsalted
1 teaspoon salt	butter, melted
½ cup plus 1 tablespoon	
wheat germ	

Preheat the oven to 375° F. Lightly coat a 9 × 5 × 2½ inch loaf pan with nonstick cooking spray.

In a large bowl, sift together the flour, baking soda, baking powder, and salt. Add ½ cup of the wheat germ and mix well. In a small bowl whisk together the yogurt, molasses, and butter, then stir into the dry ingredients just until they are moistened, about 10 strokes.

Spoon the batter into the pan and sprinkle with remaining wheat germ. Bake for 40 to 50 minutes, or until light golden brown and a wooden skewer inserted in the loaf's center comes out clean.

Cool for 10 minutes in the baking pan. Remove from the pan and serve warm or transfer to a wire rack to cool completely.

MAKES 12 SLICES
Per slice: 183 cal. (18% from fat), 3.8 g. fat, 2.9 g. fiber

Carrot-Nutmeg Bread with Honey-Orange Glaze

The aroma of nutmeg and carrots is irresistible to carrot-cake lovers. Serve cool, spread with low-fat cream cheese and honey.

2 cups all-purpose flour
1/2 cup sugar
1 teaspoon baking powder
1 teaspoon baking soda
1/2 teaspoon salt
1 teaspoon ground nutmeg
2 cups peeled, grated carrots
2 large eggs, lightly beaten

1/2 cup nonfat plain yogurt
1/2 cup fresh orange juice
2 tablespoons canola oil or melted unsalted butter

Honey-Orange Glaze

1/4 cup fresh orange juice
2 tablespoons honey

Preheat the oven to 375° F. Lightly coat a 9 × 5 × 2½ inch loaf pan with nonstick cooking spray.

In a large bowl, sift together the flour, sugar, baking powder, baking soda, salt, and nutmeg. Add the carrots and stir to incorporate thoroughly. In a small bowl, whisk together the eggs, yogurt, orange juice, and oil until well mixed. Stir the liquid ingredients into the dry ingredients just until the dry are moistened, about 10 strokes.

Spoon the batter into the pan. Bake 40 to 50 minutes, or until light golden brown and a skewer inserted in the center comes out clean.

To make the glaze, bring the orange juice and honey to a boil in a small saucepan over medium heat, stirring until smooth. When the bread is done, brush the warm top with the glaze.

Cool for 10 minutes in the baking pan. Remove from the pan and serve warm or transfer to a wire rack to cool completely.

MAKES 12 SLICES
Per slice: 165 cal. (17% from fat), 3.1 g. fat, 1.2 g. fiber

Chocolate-Cinnamon Bread

Make this sinfully good bread a day ahead for the best flavor.

2 cups all-purpose flour
3/4 cup sugar
1 tablespoon unsweetened dark cocoa powder
2 teaspoons ground cinnamon
1 teaspoon espresso coffee powder
1 teaspoon salt
1 teaspoon baking powder
1 1/2 teaspoons baking soda
1/3 cup semisweet chocolate chips

1 large egg, lightly beaten
2 large egg whites, lightly beaten
1 cup nonfat buttermilk
2 tablespoons unsalted butter, melted

Cocoa Dusting

1 tablespoon confectioners' sugar
1 teaspoon ground cinnamon
1 teaspoon unsweetened dark cocoa powder

Preheat the oven to 375° F. Lightly coat a 9 × 5 × 2½ inch loaf pan with nonstick cooking spray.

In a large bowl, sift together the flour, sugar, cocoa, cinnamon, espresso powder, salt, baking powder, and baking soda. Blend in the chocolate chips. In a small bowl, whisk together the egg, egg whites, buttermilk, and butter. Stir into the dry ingredients just until the dry are moistened. Spoon the batter into the pan. Bake 45 to 55 minutes, or until light brown and a skewer inserted in the center comes out clean.

Cool for 10 minutes in the pan. Mix the confectioners' sugar, cinnamon, and cocoa powder and sprinkle over the loaf. Remove from the pan and serve or cool on a wire rack.

MAKES 12 SLICES
Per slice: 180 cal. (21% from fat), 4.2 g. fat, 1.4 g. fiber

Honey-Almond Bread

Honey seasoned with lemon and thyme has moisture and a wonderful herbal taste. Refrigerated, the infused honey will keep for about six months. Thin slices spread with lemon curd or jam go well with herbal tea, and thicker slices topped with low-fat yogurt make an excellent dessert.

Lemon-Thyme Honey

1 cup honey
1 tablespoon coarsely grated lemon zest
3 tablespoons fresh lemon juice
$\frac{1}{3}$ cup fresh thyme leaves

2 cups whole wheat flour
$\frac{1}{3}$ cup dark brown sugar

2 teaspoons baking powder
1 teaspoon ground allspice
1 teaspoon ground cinnamon
$\frac{1}{2}$ teaspoon salt
2 large eggs, lightly beaten
$\frac{1}{4}$ cup fresh orange juice
3 tablespoons unsalted butter, melted
$\frac{1}{4}$ cup finely chopped almonds

Preheat the oven to 350° F. Lightly coat a 9 × 5 × 2½ inch loaf pan with nonstick cooking spray.

To make the lemon-thyme honey, in a medium saucepan combine the honey, lemon zest, lemon juice, and thyme leaves. Place over medium heat and simmer for 5 minutes. Remove, let cool to room temperature, and strain through a fine sieve.

In a large bowl, sift together the flour, sugar, baking powder, allspice, cinnamon, and salt. In a small bowl, whisk together the eggs, $\frac{3}{4}$ cup of the lemon-thyme honey, orange juice, and butter until well mixed. Stir the liquid ingredients into the dry ingredients just until the dry are moistened, about 10 strokes.

Spoon the batter into the loaf pan and sprinkle the top with the chopped almonds. Bake for 50 to 60 minutes, or until golden brown and a wooden skewer inserted in the center of the loaf comes out clean. When the bread is done, brush the top with the remaining honey.

Cool for 10 minutes in the baking pan. Remove from the pan and serve warm or transfer to a wire rack to cool completely.

MAKES 12 SLICES
Per slice: 229 cal. (21% from fat), 5.6 g. fat, 2.8 g. fiber

Maple-Cranberry Corn Bread

Sweet maple syrup and tart cranberries guarantee this bread will be an instant family favorite—especially when served at a Thanksgiving or holiday meal.

1 cup yellow cornmeal
1½ cups all-purpose flour
3 teaspoons baking powder
½ teaspoon salt
2 large eggs, lightly beaten
1 cup skim milk
¾ cup plus 1 tablespoon pure
  maple syrup

4 tablespoons unsalted
  butter, melted
1 cup fresh or frozen and
  thawed cranberries,
  coarsely chopped

Preheat the oven to 375° F. Lightly coat a 9 × 5 × 2½ inch loaf pan with nonstick cooking spray.

In a large bowl, sift together the cornmeal, flour, baking powder, and salt. In a small bowl, whisk together the eggs, milk, ¾ cup of the maple syrup, and butter. Stir the liquid ingredients into the dry ingredients just until the dry are moistened, about 10 strokes. Lightly fold in the chopped cranberries.

Spoon the batter into the loaf pan and bake for 45 to 55 minutes, or until light golden and a wooden skewer inserted in the center of the loaf comes out clean.

Cool for 10 minutes in the pan and brush with the remaining 1 tablespoon of maple syrup. Serve warm or transfer to a wire rack to cool completely.

MAKES 12 SLICES
Per slice: 186 cal. (25% from fat), 5.2 g. fat, 1.4 g. fiber

Oatmeal-Raisin Bread

Raisins replace the need for excess fat and enable the bread to remain moist for several days after baking. With the oats, they are an excellent source of added fiber.

1 cup raisins	3 teaspoons baking powder
1 cup water	$^{1}/_{4}$ teaspoon salt
2 tablespoons unsalted butter	1 cup plus 1 tablespoon old-
1 cup all-purpose flour	fashioned rolled oats
$^{1}/_{4}$ cup sugar	2 large eggs, lightly beaten

Preheat the oven to 375° F. Lightly coat a 9 × 5 × 2½ inch loaf pan with nonstick cooking spray.

Combine the raisins and water in a small saucepan and simmer over medium heat for 3 minutes, or until the raisins are plumped. Remove from the heat, add the butter, and stir until melted. Let cool. Do not drain.

In a large bowl, sift together the flour, sugar, baking powder, and salt. Add 1 cup of the oats and stir to incorporate thoroughly. Whisk the eggs into the cooled raisin mixture. Stir the liquid ingredients into the dry ingredients just until the dry are moistened, about 10 strokes.

Spoon the batter into the loaf pan and sprinkle the top with the remaining 1 tablespoon of oats. Bake for 45 to 55 minutes, or until light golden brown and a wooden skewer inserted in the center of the loaf comes out clean.

Cool for 10 minutes in the baking pan. Remove from the pan and serve warm or transfer to a wire rack to cool completely.

MAKES 12 SLICES
Per slice: 147 cal. (20% from fat), 3.3 g. fat, 1.5 g. fiber

Spiced Prune Bread

Homemade prune butter is spicy and delicious, while very nutritious and low in fat. Refrigerated, the prune butter will keep for about three months.

This bread will keep well because the pureed prunes make it so moist. Another plus is that it's very high in fiber.

1 cup all-purpose flour
$\frac{1}{2}$ cup whole wheat flour
$\frac{1}{2}$ cup sugar
$1\frac{1}{2}$ teaspoons baking soda
$\frac{1}{2}$ teaspoon salt

2 large eggs, lightly beaten
$1\frac{1}{2}$ cups Prune Butter (recipe follows)
3 tablespoons canola oil or melted unsalted butter

Preheat the oven to 375° F. Lightly coat a 9 × 5 × 2½ inch loaf pan with nonstick cooking spray.

In a large bowl, sift together the all-purpose and whole wheat flours, sugar, baking soda, and salt. In a small bowl, whisk together the eggs, Prune Butter, and oil. Stir the liquid ingredients into the dry ingredients just until the dry are moistened; use about 10 strokes.

Spoon the batter into the loaf pan. Bake for 50 to 60 minutes, or until golden brown and a wooden skewer inserted in the center of the loaf comes out clean.

Cool for 10 minutes in the baking pan. Remove from the pan and serve warm or transfer to a wire rack to cool completely.

MAKES 12 SLICES
Per slice: 215 cal. (22% from fat), 5.5 g. fat, 4.0 g. fiber

Prune Butter

2 cups pitted prunes
1 cup water
¼ teaspoon salt
½ teaspoon ground
  cinnamon

¼ teaspoon ground allspice
¼ teaspoon ground cloves
2 tablespoons cider vinegar
1 tablespoon unsalted butter

In a 1-quart saucepan, combine the prunes, water, salt, cinnamon, allspice, and cloves and simmer over medium heat for 15 to 20 minutes, or until the prunes are plumped and the liquid has reduced to about half. Place the mixture in a blender or food processor and process until smooth, adding the vinegar and butter while continuing to process. Cool and store refrigerated in an airtight container.

MAKES ABOUT 2 CUPS

Pumpkin-Maple Bread

If you are planning brunch, this bread makes a fragrant and sweet French toast when topped with bananas and blueberries. It is equally delicious plain with a freshly brewed cup of coffee.

1½ cups all-purpose flour
1 teaspoon ground cinnamon
1 teaspoon ground allspice
1 teaspoon ground cloves
1 teaspoon ground nutmeg
½ teaspoon salt
1 teaspoon baking powder

1 teaspoon baking soda
2 large eggs, lightly beaten
¾ cup pure maple syrup
1 cup fresh or canned
   pumpkin puree
¼ cup dried cranberries or
   currants

Preheat the oven to 375° F. Lightly coat a 9 × 5 × 2½ inch loaf pan with nonstick cooking spray.

In a large bowl sift together the flour, cinnamon, allspice, cloves, nutmeg, salt, baking powder, and baking soda. In a small bowl whisk together the eggs, maple syrup, and pumpkin until well mixed. Stir the liquid ingredients into the dry ingredients just until the dry are moistened, about 10 strokes.

Spoon the batter into the loaf pan, sprinkle the top with the cranberries, and lightly press them into the batter. Bake for 50 to 60 minutes, or until light golden brown and a wooden skewer inserted in the center of the loaf comes out clean. If the cranberries start to burn, loosely cover the pan with aluminum foil and continue baking.

Cool for 10 minutes in the baking pan. Remove from the pan and serve warm or transfer to a wire rack to cool completely.

MAKES 12 SLICES
Per slice: 117 cal. (9% from fat), 1.2 g. fat, 1.5 g. fiber

Snack Breads

Pumpernickel-Fig Skillet Bread

Bake this rich bread to serve warm, in wedges right out of the skillet, with a cold fruit salad.

3 tablespoons yellow
cornmeal, plus extra
for dusting pan
1½ cups coarsely chopped
fresh figs or 1 cup
dried figs
2 cups rye flour

1 tablespoon baking powder
1½ teaspoons salt
1½ cups skim milk
¼ cup blackstrap molasses
2 tablespoons safflower or
corn oil

Preheat oven to 375° F. Lightly coat a 9- or 10-inch-diameter heavy ovenproof skillet with nonstick cooking spray and dust with cornmeal.

For dried figs, place a small saucepan over medium heat with ½ cup of water and simmer for 10 minutes. Let cool. Drain and chop coarsely.

In a large bowl, sift together the cornmeal, rye flour, baking powder, and salt. In a small bowl, whisk together the milk, molasses, and oil until well mixed. Stir the liquid ingredients into the dry ingredients, about 15 strokes. The dough should be fairly stiff and evenly moistened. Gently fold in the chopped figs.

Spoon the dough into the prepared skillet, and using wet fingers, pat out the dough gently to fill the skillet and distribute it evenly. Bake for 20 to 30 minutes, or until the bread is firm and a wooden skewer inserted in the center of the loaf comes out clean.

Cool for 10 minutes and remove from the pan. Serve warm.

MAKES 12 SLICES
Per slice: 133 cal. (18% from fat), 2.7 g. fat, 3.4 g. fiber

Date—Sunflower Seed Bread

Encrusted with a crunchy seed topping, this bread makes for a healthy, summery snack when served with fresh fruit and iced tea at a barbecue or picnic.

$\frac{1}{2}$ cup all-purpose flour
$\frac{3}{4}$ cup whole wheat flour
$\frac{1}{2}$ teaspoon baking powder
2 teaspoons baking soda
$\frac{1}{2}$ teaspoon salt
$\frac{1}{4}$ cup oat bran
1 large egg, lightly beaten

$\frac{1}{2}$ cup honey
$\frac{3}{4}$ cup low-fat buttermilk
$\frac{1}{4}$ cup sunflower or canola oil
1 cup chopped dates
$\frac{1}{4}$ cup coarsely chopped
    sunflower seeds

Preheat the oven to 375° F. Lightly coat a 9 × 5 × 2½ inch loaf pan with nonstick cooking spray.

In a large bowl, sift together the all-purpose and whole wheat flours, baking powder, baking soda, and salt. Add the oat bran and stir to incorporate thoroughly. In a small bowl, whisk together the egg, honey, buttermilk, and oil until well mixed. Stir the liquid ingredients into the dry ingredients just until the dry are moistened, about 10 strokes. Gently fold in the chopped dates. Spoon the batter into the loaf pan and sprinkle the top of the bread with the sunflower seeds. Bake for 45 to 55 minutes, or until light golden brown and a wooden skewer inserted in the center of the loaf comes out clean.

Cool for 10 minutes in the baking pan. Remove from the pan and serve warm or transfer to a wire rack to cool completely.

MAKES 12 SLICES
Per slice: 200 cal. (29% from fat), 7.0 g. fat, 2.6 g. fiber

Zesty Citrus Bread

For the ultimate peanut butter and jelly sandwich, try this bread with orange marmalade instead of jelly.

1 medium orange, scrubbed and dried	1 cup all-purpose flour
1 medium lemon, scrubbed and dried	$\frac{1}{2}$ teaspoon baking powder
1 medium lime, scrubbed and dried	2 teaspoons baking soda
1 cup sugar	$\frac{1}{2}$ teaspoon salt
1 cup old-fashioned rolled oats	2 large eggs, lightly beaten
	1 cup nonfat plain yogurt
	3 tablespoons canola oil or melted unsalted butter

Preheat the oven to 375° F. Lightly coat a 9 × 5 × 2½ inch loaf pan with nonstick cooking spray.

Peel the orange, lemon, and lime with a vegetable peeler, removing only the zest, not the white pith. Pulse the zest, sugar, and oats in a food processor until finely chopped, about 1 minute. Squeeze the juice of the 3 fruits into a bowl and strain. Process with the oat mixture until creamy, about 30 seconds.

In a large bowl, sift together the flour, baking powder, baking soda, and salt. In a small bowl, whisk together the eggs, yogurt, and oil until well mixed, combine with the oat mixture, and mix well. Stir the liquid ingredients into the dry ingredients just until the dry are moistened, about 15 strokes. Spoon the batter into the pan and bake 45 to 55 minutes, or until light brown and a skewer inserted in the center comes out clean. Cool for 10 minutes in the baking pan. Serve warm or cool on a wire rack.

MAKES 12 SLICES
Per slice: 190 cal. (23% from fat), 4.8 g. fat, 1.1 g. fiber

Fresh Ginger—Orange Bread

This peppery bread is delicious with afternoon tea. Also try it with lemon juice and zest, but use only one-quarter cup juice.

1¾ cups all-purpose flour
¾ cup sugar
2 teaspoons baking powder
½ teaspoon salt
2 tablespoons grated orange zest
2 large eggs, lightly beaten
½ cup fresh orange juice
½ cup skim milk
¼ cup honey

3 tablespoons unsalted butter, melted
2-inch piece of ginger, peeled and coarsely grated

Orange-Ginger Glaze

2 tablespoons orange marmalade
1 tablespoon water
1 teaspoon ground ginger

Preheat the oven to 375° F. Lightly coat a 9 × 5 × 2½ inch loaf pan with nonstick cooking spray.

In a large bowl, sift together the flour, sugar, baking powder, and salt. Add the orange zest and mix well. In a small bowl, whisk together the eggs, orange juice, milk, honey, butter, and ginger until well mixed, then stir into the dry ingredients just until they are moistened, about 10 strokes. Spoon the batter into the pan and bake for 45 to 55 minutes, or until light brown and a wooden skewer inserted in the center of the loaf comes out clean.

To make the glaze, combine the marmalade, water, and ginger in a small saucepan and bring to a boil over medium heat. When the bread is done, brush the warm top with the glaze. Cool for 10 minutes in the baking pan. Serve warm or cool on a wire rack.

MAKES 12 SLICES
Per slice: 189 cal. (18% from fat), 3.9 g. fat, 0.7 g. fiber

Fruitcake Bread

What could taste better midafternoon than a fresh, moist slice of fruit bread? Serve warm with fruit preserves and a dab of low-fat sour cream.

$\frac{1}{2}$ cup golden raisins
$\frac{1}{2}$ cup chopped dates
$\frac{1}{2}$ cup dried apricots, chopped
$1\frac{1}{2}$ cups water
1 cup all-purpose flour
1 cup whole wheat flour
$\frac{1}{2}$ cup dark brown sugar

$1\frac{1}{2}$ teaspoons baking powder
$\frac{1}{2}$ teaspoon baking soda
$\frac{1}{2}$ teaspoon salt
1 large egg, lightly beaten
4 tablespoons canola oil or melted unsalted butter
$\frac{1}{2}$ cup low-fat buttermilk

Combine the raisins, dates, apricots, and 1 cup of the water in a small saucepan and simmer over medium heat for 10 minutes, until the fruits are plumped. Drain and cool.

Preheat the oven to 375° F. Lightly coat a $9 \times 5 \times 2\frac{1}{2}$ inch loaf pan with nonstick cooking spray.

In a large bowl, sift together the flours, sugar, baking powder, baking soda, and salt. In a small bowl, whisk together the egg, oil, buttermilk, and water until well mixed. Stir the liquid ingredients into the dry ingredients just until the dry are moistened, about 10 strokes. Gently fold in the cooked fruits. Spoon the batter into the pan and bake 45 to 55 minutes, or until light brown and a wooden skewer inserted in the center comes out clean.

Cool for 10 minutes in the baking pan. Remove from the pan and serve warm or transfer to a wire rack to cool completely.

MAKES 12 SLICES
Per slice: 197 cal. (24% from fat), 5.5 g. fat, 2.6 g. fiber

Wheat-Free Brown Rice and Raisin Bread

Rice flour and potato starch can be found in most health-food stores, and replace whole the whole wheat flours for a gluten-free bread. This is best accompanying a thick, chunky soup or a stir-fry.

1 cup brown-rice flour
$\frac{1}{2}$ cup potato starch
2 teaspoons baking powder
1 teaspoon baking soda
$\frac{1}{2}$ teaspoon salt
1 cup cooked brown rice

1 cup dark raisins
1 cup warm water
2 large eggs, lightly beaten
3 tablespoons unsalted
    butter, melted

Preheat the oven to 375° F. Lightly coat a 9 × 5 × 2½ inch loaf pan with nonstick cooking spray.

In a large bowl, sift together the flour, potato starch, baking powder, baking soda, and salt. Combine the rice, raisins, and water in a food processor and blend until the mixture is smooth, about 2 minutes. Add the eggs and butter and continue processing until well mixed. Scrape the mixture into the dry ingredients and stir just until the dry are moistened; use about 10 strokes. Spoon the batter into the loaf pan and bake for 45 to 55 minutes, or until golden brown and a wooden skewer inserted in the center of the loaf comes out clean.

Cool for 10 minutes in the baking pan. Remove from the pan and serve warm or transfer to a wire rack to cool completely.

MAKES 12 SLICES
Per slice: 171 cal. (22% from fat), 4.3 g. fat, 1.8 g. fiber

Traditional Irish Soda Bread

Freshly baked soda bread is very heart-healthy, since it's egg-free. Serve it warm with soup and a crisp green salad, or toasted with Apricot-Lemon Spread (see page 88).

1 cup plus 1 tablespoon
   all-purpose flour
1 cup whole wheat flour
$^1/_2$ cup sugar
1 teaspoon baking powder
1 teaspoon baking soda
$^1/_2$ teaspoon salt

$^1/_2$ cup golden raisins,
   coarsely chopped
2 teaspoons caraway seeds
1 cup nonfat buttermilk
$^1/_4$ cup canola oil or melted
   unsalted butter

Preheat the oven to 350° F. In a large bowl, sift together 1 cup of the all-purpose flour and the whole wheat flour, sugar, baking powder, baking soda, and salt. Add the raisins and caraway seeds and stir to incorporate thoroughly. In a small bowl, whisk together the buttermilk and oil until blended. Stir the liquid ingredients into the dry ingredients just until the dry are moistened and a batter forms, about 10 strokes. Turn the dough out onto a lightly floured surface and knead for 1 to 2 minutes. Shape into a ball and place in an ungreased 10-inch ovenproof skillet. Using a sharp knife, slash a large × shape in the top of the dough. Sprinkle the top with the remaining 1 tablespoon of flour. Bake for 35 to 40 minutes, or until light golden brown. The loaf should sound hollow when the bottom is tapped.

Cool for 10 minutes in the baking pan. Remove from the pan and serve warm or transfer to a wire rack to cool completely.

MAKES 12 SLICES
Per slice: 171 cal. (26% from fat), 5.0 g. fat, 1.8 g. fiber

Orange-Bran Bread

Make a child's school lunch with this wholesome bran bread that's studded with raisins—and then make one for yourself!

3/4 cup golden raisins
1 cup fresh orange juice
1½ cups all-purpose flour
3 tablespoons sugar
3 teaspoons baking powder
½ teaspoon salt

2 teaspoons grated orange zest
½ cup bran
1 large egg, lightly beaten
½ cup water

Preheat the oven to 375° F. Lightly coat a 9 × 5 × 2½ inch loaf pan with nonstick cooking spray.

Combine the raisins and orange juice in a small saucepan and simmer over medium heat for 2 minutes, or until the raisins are plumped. Remove from the heat and let cool. Do not drain. In a blender or food processor with a steel blade, puree the raisin mixture until smooth.

In a large bowl, sift together the flour, sugar, baking powder, and salt. Add the orange zest and bran and mix thoroughly. In a small bowl, whisk together the egg, water, and raisin puree until well mixed. Stir the liquid ingredients into the dry ingredients just until the dry are moistened, about 10 strokes.

Spoon the batter into the loaf pan and bake for 45 to 55 minutes, or until light golden brown and a wooden skewer inserted in the center of the loaf comes out clean.

Cool for 10 minutes in the baking pan. Remove from the pan and serve warm or transfer to a wire rack to cool completely.

MAKES 12 SLICES
Per slice: 121 cal. (6% from fat), 0.8 g. fat, 2.8 g. fiber

Persimmon Bread with Orange Glaze

Persimmon adds a tangy but sweet flavor to this bread, which is especially good when served warm with a low-fat, mild cheese such as goat's milk or Swiss. Before being pureed, persimmons must be peeled (a simple vegetable peeler works well) and the seeds removed.

1¼ cup all-purpose flour
¼ cup sugar
1 teaspoon baking powder
2 teaspoons baking soda
½ teaspoon salt
1 teaspoon ground nutmeg
½ teaspoon ground allspice
¾ cup wheat germ
1 large egg, lightly beaten
1 cup peeled and pureed
   persimmons

¾ cup low-fat buttermilk
½ cup water
2 tablespoons vegetable
   or corn oil

Orange Glaze

2 tablespoons orange
   marmalade
1 teaspoon grated orange zest

Preheat the oven to 375° F. Lightly coat a 9 × 5 × 2½ inch loaf pan with nonstick cooking spray.

In a large bowl, sift together the flour, sugar, baking powder, baking soda, salt, nutmeg, and allspice. Add the wheat germ and mix thoroughly. In a small bowl, whisk together the egg, persimmon puree, buttermilk, water, and oil until well mixed. Stir the liquid ingredients into the dry ingredients just until the dry are moistened, about 10 strokes.

Spoon the batter into the loaf pan and bake for 45 to 55 minutes, or until light golden brown and a wooden skewer inserted in the center of the loaf comes out clean.

To make the glaze, while the bread is baking, combine the orange marmalade and zest in a small saucepan and warm over low heat. When the bread is done and still warm, brush the top with the glaze, until all is used.

Cool for 10 minutes in the baking pan. Remove from the pan and serve warm or transfer to a wire rack to cool completely.

MAKES 12 SLICES
Per slice: 134 cal. (25% from fat), 3.8 g. fat, 1.5 g. fiber

Pineapple Bread with Crunchy Walnut Topping

Serve this sweet and spicy bread warm as a low-fat replacement for doughnuts.

1¾ cups whole wheat flour
¾ cup light brown sugar
1½ teaspoons baking powder
1 teaspoon baking soda
1 teaspoon salt
1 teaspoon ground cinnamon
½ teaspoon ground nutmeg
¼ teaspoon ground allspice
2 large eggs, lightly beaten
1 tablespoon grated lemon zest
¼ cup fresh lemon juice
¾ cup low-fat buttermilk

2 tablespoons unsalted butter, melted
1 cup ¼-inch diced fresh pineapple

Crunchy Walnut Topping

1 tablespoon unsalted butter, melted
2 tablespoons wheat germ
1 tablespoon light brown sugar
1 tablespoon chopped walnuts

Preheat the oven to 375° F. Lightly coat a 9 × 5 × 2½ inch loaf pan with nonstick cooking spray.

In a large bowl, sift together the flour, sugar, baking powder, baking soda, salt, cinnamon, nutmeg, and allspice. In a small bowl, whisk together the eggs, lemon zest, lemon juice, buttermilk, and butter. Add ¾ cup of the diced pineapple. Stir the liquid ingredients into the dry ingredients just until the dry are moistened, about 10 strokes. Spoon the batter into the loaf pan and arrange the remaining pineapple on top.

To make the topping, mix together the butter, wheat germ,

brown sugar, and walnuts in a small bowl. Sprinkle over the bread evenly and lightly press the topping into the batter. Bake for 45 to 55 minutes, or until light golden brown and a wooden skewer inserted in the center of the loaf comes out clean. If the pineapple topping starts to burn, loosely cover the pan with aluminum foil and continue baking.

Cool for 10 minutes in the baking pan. Remove from the pan and serve warm or transfer to a wire rack to cool completely.

MAKES 12 SLICES

Per slice: 173 cal. (23% from fat), 4.6 g. fat, 2.6 g. fiber

Sweet Potato Bread

Round out a meal of grilled meat and vegetables with this bread, which is so satisfying that it is almost a meal by itself.

³/₄ cup whole wheat flour
½ cup all-purpose flour
³/₄ cup light brown sugar
2 teaspoons baking powder
1 teaspoon salt
1 teaspoon ground cinnamon
2 large eggs, lightly beaten
2 cups mashed cooked sweet
   potatoes
3 teaspoons grated lemon
   zest

1 tablespoon fresh lemon
   juice
1 cup skim milk
4 tablespoons unsalted
   butter, melted

Lemon-Cinnamon Topping

1 teaspoon grated lemon zest
½ teaspoon ground
   cinnamon
1 teaspoon light brown sugar

Preheat the oven to 375° F. Lightly coat a 9 × 5 × 2½ inch loaf pan with nonstick cooking spray.

In a large bowl, sift together the flours, sugar, baking powder, salt, and cinnamon. In a small bowl, whisk together the eggs, potatoes, lemon zest, lemon juice, skim milk, and butter until well mixed, then stir into the dry ingredients just until the dry are moistened, about 10 strokes. Spoon the batter into the pan.

For the topping, mix together the lemon zest, cinnamon, and brown sugar. Sprinkle over the bread evenly and lightly press it into the batter. Bake 45 to 55 minutes, or until light brown and a wooden skewer inserted in the center comes out clean. Cool for 10 minutes in the pan. Serve warm or cool on a wire rack.

MAKES 12 SLICES
Per slice: 189 cal. (23% from fat), 5.0 g. fat, 2.5 g. fiber

Whole Wheat—Oat Bread

Dense with goodness, and with a coarse texture, this bread toasts up beautifully for any meal.

1 cup whole wheat flour
$\frac{1}{2}$ cup sugar
$\frac{1}{2}$ teaspoon baking powder
$1\frac{1}{2}$ teaspoons baking soda
$\frac{1}{2}$ teaspoon salt
$1\frac{1}{2}$ cups plus 1 tablespoon
    quick rolled oats

1 large egg, lightly beaten
1 cup low-fat buttermilk
3 tablespoons unsalted
    butter, melted

Preheat the oven to 375° F. Lightly coat a 9 × 5 × 2½ inch loaf pan with nonstick cooking spray.

In a large bowl, sift together the flour, sugar, baking powder, baking soda, and salt. Add 1½ cups of the oats and stir to incorporate thoroughly. In a small bowl, whisk together the egg, buttermilk, and butter until well mixed. Stir the liquid ingredients into the dry ingredients just until the dry are moistened, about 10 strokes.

Spoon the batter into the loaf pan and sprinkle the top with the remaining 1 tablespoon of oats. Bake for 45 to 55 minutes, or until light golden brown and a wooden skewer inserted in the center of the loaf comes out clean.

Cool for 10 minutes in the baking pan. Remove from the pan and serve warm or transfer to a wire rack to cool completely.

MAKES 12 SLICES
Per slice: 145 cal. (26% from fat), 4.3 g. fat, 2.1 g. fiber

Savory Zucchini Bread

Morning coffee and afternoon tea are perfect times to savor this bread, which has a hint of apple flavor. Toast thick slices and serve with some Mango Chutney (see page 90) or with fresh fruit salsa.

1¼ cups all-purpose flour
½ cup whole wheat flour
1 cup brown sugar
1 teaspoon baking powder
1 teaspoon baking soda
½ teaspoon salt
2 teaspoons ground cinnamon

¼ teaspoon ground nutmeg
2 large eggs, lightly beaten
1 cup unsweetened apple-sauce
2 cups grated zucchini
3 tablespoons corn oil
1 tablespoon coarsely chopped pecans

Preheat the oven to 375° F. Lightly coat a 9 × 5 × 2½ inch loaf pan with nonstick cooking spray.

In a large bowl, sift together the all-purpose and whole wheat flours, sugar, baking powder, baking soda, salt, cinnamon, and nutmeg. In a small bowl, whisk together the eggs, applesauce, zucchini, and oil until well mixed. Stir the liquid ingredients into the dry ingredients just until the dry are moistened, about 10 strokes. Spoon the batter into the loaf pan and sprinkle the top of the bread with the chopped pecans. Bake for 45 to 55 minutes, or until light golden brown and a wooden skewer inserted in the center of the loaf comes out clean.

Cool for 10 minutes in the baking pan. Remove from the pan and serve warm or transfer to a wire rack to cool completely.

MAKES 12 SLICES
Per slice: 169 cal. (28% from fat), 5.3 g. fat, 1.7 g. fiber

Fat-Free Breads

Brown Sugar Beer Bread

Unlike traditional beer bread, which can be flat and heavy, this fat-free version is fairly thick and soft. Serve alongside roasted turkey or chicken, with a baked potato and steamed vegetables.

1 cup all-purpose flour	$\frac{1}{2}$ teaspoon ground cloves
2 cups whole wheat flour	1 tablespoon grated orange zest
2 teaspoons baking powder	
1 teaspoon baking soda	1 cup dark brown sugar
$1\frac{1}{2}$ teaspoons salt	$1\frac{1}{2}$ to 2 cups dark beer

Preheat the oven to 375° F. Lightly coat a 10 × 15 inch baking sheet with nonstick cooking spray.

In a large bowl, sift together the all-purpose and whole wheat flours, baking powder, baking soda, salt, and cloves. Add the zest, brown sugar, and $1\frac{1}{2}$ cups of the beer and stir together (use 15 strokes) to make a firm dough. Add more beer if necessary; the dough should be quite wet. Moisten your hands and knead the dough gently on a floured work surface for about 3 minutes, until the dough is smooth and uniform in consistency. Shape into a round loaf, and place on the baking sheet. Cut a $\frac{1}{2}$-inch-deep × across the top of the loaf using a sharp knife. Bake for 35 to 45 minutes, or until the loaf is nicely browned and has a hollow sound when tapped on the bottom.

Cool for 10 minutes on the baking sheet. Remove from the pan and serve warm or transfer to a wire rack to cool completely.

MAKES 12 SLICES
Per slice: 160 cal., less than 1.0 g. fat, 2.7 g. fiber

Buckwheat-Caraway Bread

Buckwheat flour has a slightly nutty flavor. This bread is a great companion for marinated herring, or salads with a tart vinegar flavor.

1 cup buckwheat flour
2 teaspoons baking powder
$\frac{1}{2}$ teaspoon salt
$\frac{1}{4}$ teaspoon freshly ground
    black pepper
$\frac{1}{2}$ cup quick rolled oats

$1\frac{1}{2}$ teaspoons caraway seeds
1 cup thinly sliced scallions,
    white and green parts
2 large egg whites, lightly
    beaten
1 cup skim milk

Preheat the oven to 375° F. Lightly coat an 8 × 8 inch baking pan with nonstick cooking spray.

In a large bowl, sift together the flour, baking powder, salt, and pepper. Add the oats, 1 teaspoon of the caraway seeds, and scallions and stir to incorporate thoroughly. In a small bowl, whisk together the egg whites and milk until well mixed. Stir the liquid ingredients into the dry ingredients just until the dry are moistened, about 10 strokes.

Spoon the batter into the baking pan and sprinkle with the remaining $\frac{1}{2}$ teaspoon caraway seeds. Bake for 20 minutes, or until golden brown and a wooden skewer inserted in the center of the loaf comes out clean.

Cool for 10 minutes in the baking pan. Remove from the pan and serve warm or transfer to a wire rack to cool completely.

MAKES 12 SLICES
Per slice: 67 cal., less than 1.0 g. fat, 1.9 g. fiber

Butternut Squash Bread

Butternut squash is so abundant at farm stands in the fall months. Serve this bread warm with a bean soup or cube, toast, and serve as croutons in a green bean salad.

1 cup all-purpose flour
3 teaspoons baking powder
$\frac{1}{2}$ teaspoon salt
1 teaspoon ground cinnamon
$\frac{1}{4}$ teaspoon ground allspice
$\frac{1}{4}$ teaspoon ground nutmeg
$\frac{1}{2}$ cup plus 1 tablespoon
  wheat germ

$\frac{1}{2}$ cup oat bran
1 tablespoon grated orange
  zest
4 large egg whites
2 cups mashed cooked
  butternut squash
$\frac{1}{2}$ cup honey
$\frac{1}{2}$ cup fresh orange juice

Preheat the oven to 375° F. Lightly coat a 9 × 5 × 2$\frac{1}{2}$ inch loaf pan with nonstick cooking spray.

In a large bowl, sift together the flour, baking powder, salt, cinnamon, allspice, and nutmeg. Add $\frac{1}{2}$ cup of the wheat germ, the oat bran, and zest and stir to incorporate thoroughly. In a small bowl, whisk together the egg whites, squash, honey, and orange juice until well mixed. Stir the liquid ingredients into the dry ingredients just until the dry are moistened, about 10 strokes.

Spoon the batter into the loaf pan and sprinkle with the remaining 1 tablespoon wheat germ. Bake for 45 to 55 minutes, or until golden brown and a wooden skewer inserted in the center of the loaf comes out clean.

Cool for 10 minutes in the baking pan. Remove from the pan and serve warm or transfer to a wire rack to cool completely.

MAKES 12 SLICES
Per slice: 133 cal., less than 1.0 g. fat, 2.9 g. fiber

Campfire Bread

During my childhood we took weekend camping trips and would prepare this quick and easy bread as a nighttime snack. After the bread had baked for fifteen or twenty minutes, if you put your hand on top of it and it was hot, you knew it was done. Baked in a skillet, the bread is crusty and chewy. Substitute diced bananas or diced apples if blueberries are not in season.

1½ cups whole wheat flour
1½ cups all-purpose flour
3 teaspoons baking powder
1 teaspoon salt

½ cup sugar
1½ cups fresh blueberries
1½ to 2 cups water

Preheat the oven to 400° F. Lightly coat a 9-inch heavy ovenproof skillet with nonstick cooking spray. In a large bowl, sift together the whole wheat and all-purpose flours, baking powder, salt, and sugar. Measure 1 tablespoon of the mixture in a small bowl and add the blueberries. Toss lightly until the blueberries are coated with the flour mixture, and set aside. Stir the water into the dry ingredients just until the dry are moistened, about 10 strokes. Gently fold in the blueberries. The dough should be stiff and evenly moistened.

Spoon the batter into the skillet and, using wet hands, pat out the batter to distribute the batter evenly in the skillet. Bake for 25 to 35 minutes, until the bread is firm to the touch, golden brown, and a wooden skewer inserted in the center comes out clean.

Cool for 10 minutes in the skillet. Remove from the pan and serve warm or transfer to a wire rack to cool completely.

MAKES 12 SLICES
Per slice: 145 cal., less than 1.0 g. fat, 2.7 g. fiber

Five-Grain Bread

Increasingly popular because of its taste and nutritional content, this fat-free multigrain bread is ideal as a light lunch with smoked turkey slices and mustard. The bread is very dense and when cubed and toasted makes excellent croutons for a Caesar salad.

$^1/_2$ cup whole wheat flour
$^1/_2$ cup buckwheat flour
$^1/_2$ cup rye flour
2 teaspoons baking powder
$^1/_2$ teaspoon baking soda
$^1/_2$ teaspoon salt
$^1/_2$ cup quick rolled oats
$^1/_2$ cup oat bran

$^1/_2$ cup raisins
3 large egg whites, lightly beaten
1 cup honey
1 cup unsweetened applesauce
$^1/_2$ cup skim milk

Preheat the oven to 375° F. Lightly coat a 9 × 5 × 2½ inch loaf pan with nonstick cooking spray.

In a large bowl, sift together the whole wheat, buckwheat, and rye flours, baking powder, baking soda, and salt. Add the oats, oat bran, and raisins and stir to incorporate thoroughly. In a small bowl, whisk together the egg whites, honey, applesauce, and milk until well mixed. Stir the liquid ingredients into the dry ingredients just until the dry are moistened, about 10 strokes.

Spoon the batter into the loaf pan and bake for 30 to 40 minutes, or until golden brown and a wooden skewer inserted in the center of the loaf comes out clean.

Cool for 10 minutes in the baking pan. Remove from the pan and serve warm or transfer to a wire rack to cool completely.

MAKES 12 SLICES
Per slice: 194 cal., less than 1.0 g. fat, 3.0 g. fiber

High-Fiber Bread

Coarse and crumbly, with a touch of honey, this bread has a heaping portion of many nutrients. It's delicious with Beet-Onion Preserve (see page 89).

1 cup cooked black beans, rinsed and drained
1 cup skim milk
$\frac{1}{2}$ cup barley flour
$\frac{1}{2}$ cup whole wheat flour
3 teaspoons baking powder
$\frac{1}{2}$ teaspoon salt
$\frac{1}{2}$ cup quick rolled oats
$\frac{1}{2}$ cup bran flakes
2 large egg whites, lightly beaten
$\frac{1}{4}$ cup honey

Preheat the oven to 375° F. Lightly coat a 9 × 5 × 2½ inch loaf pan with nonstick cooking spray.

Puree the beans and milk in a blender or a food processor; process about 1 minute.

In a large bowl, sift together the barley and whole wheat flours, baking powder, and salt. Add the oats and bran flakes and stir to incorporate thoroughly. In a small bowl, whisk together the bean puree, egg whites, and honey until well mixed. Stir the liquid ingredients into the dry ingredients just until the dry are moistened, about 10 strokes.

Spoon the batter into the loaf pan and bake for 40 to 50 minutes, or until golden brown and a wooden skewer inserted in the center of the loaf comes out clean.

Cool for 10 minutes in the baking pan. Remove from the pan and serve warm or transfer to a wire rack to cool completely.

MAKES 12 SLICES
Per slice: 128 cal., less than 1.0 g. fat, 3.8 g. fiber

Wild Rice Bread

Delicious with a bitter greens salad or a roasted-eggplant salad, this bread has a slightly sweet flavor and crunchy texture. Spread with Eggplant Jelly (see page 90) for additional flavor.

1 cup all-purpose flour
1 cup whole wheat flour
3 teaspoons baking powder
$\frac{1}{2}$ teaspoon salt
$\frac{1}{2}$ teaspoon freshly ground black pepper
1 cup cooked brown or wild rice

$\frac{1}{2}$ cup finely chopped onions
$\frac{1}{2}$ cup finely chopped fresh parsley
2 large egg whites, lightly beaten
$1\frac{1}{4}$ cups skim milk

Preheat the oven to 375° F. Lightly coat a 9 × 5 × 2½ inch loaf pan with nonstick cooking spray.

In a large bowl, sift together the all-purpose and whole wheat flours, baking powder, salt, and pepper. Add the rice, onions, and parsley and stir to incorporate thoroughly. In a small bowl, whisk together the egg whites and milk until well mixed. Stir the liquid ingredients into the dry ingredients just until the dry are moistened, about 10 strokes.

Spoon the batter into the loaf pan and bake for 45 to 55 minutes, or until golden brown and a wooden skewer inserted in the center of the loaf comes out clean.

Cool for 10 minutes in the baking pan. Remove from the pan and serve warm or transfer to a wire rack to cool completely.

MAKES 12 SLICES
Per slice: 100 cal., less than 1.0 g. fat, 1.9 g. fiber

Sour Cream—Cherry Bread

Dried cherries should be available in the bulk-foods aisle of your supermarket, but raisins make a good substitute. Serve this bread with fresh sour cherries or strawberries and drizzle with a fruit-flavored yogurt.

1 cup all-purpose flour
1 cup whole wheat flour
2 teaspoons baking powder
1/2 teaspoon baking soda
1/2 teaspoon salt
1 tablespoon grated lemon zest

1 cup dried cherries or raisins
4 large egg whites, lightly beaten
1 cup nonfat sour cream
1/2 cup pure maple syrup
1/4 cup fresh lemon juice

Preheat the oven to 375° F. Lightly coat a 9 × 5 × 2½ inch loaf pan with nonstick cooking spray.

In a large bowl, sift together the all-purpose and whole wheat flours, baking powder, baking soda, and salt. Add the zest and cherries and stir to incorporate thoroughly. In a small bowl, whisk together the egg whites, sour cream, maple syrup, and lemon juice until well mixed. Stir the liquid ingredients into the dry ingredients just until the dry are moistened, about 10 strokes.

Spoon the batter into the loaf pan and bake for 45 to 55 minutes, or until golden brown and a wooden skewer inserted in the center of the loaf comes out clean.

Cool for 10 minutes in the baking pan. Remove from the pan and serve warm or transfer to a wire rack to cool completely.

MAKES 12 SLICES
Per slice: 173 cal., less than 1.0 g. fat, 2.3 g. fiber

Roasted Pepper Bread

Roasted peppers have a pleasantly smoky taste and add a lot of flavor to this fat-free bread. Serve toasted in squares or wedges with savory spreads such as Ginger-Tomato Relish (see page 92).

2 medium peppers	1 teaspoon salt
1 cup plus 2 tablespoons cornmeal	$\frac{1}{2}$ cup finely chopped fresh chives
$\frac{1}{2}$ cup whole wheat flour	3 large egg whites, lightly beaten
2 teaspoons baking powder	1 cup skim milk
$\frac{1}{2}$ teaspoon baking soda	

Preheat the broiler. Lay the peppers on an ungreased baking sheet and set them about 4 inches from the flame. Turn each pepper when completely black on one side and continue until the entire pepper is black, about 4 to 8 minutes. Immediately place the peppers in a plastic bag to steam for 10 minutes. When they are cool enough to handle, remove the charred skin and seeds.

Preheat the oven to 375° F. Lightly coat an 8 × 8 inch baking pan or a 9-inch cast-iron skillet with nonstick cooking spray and sprinkle with 1 tablespoon of the cornmeal.

In a large bowl, sift together 1 cup cornmeal, the flour, baking powder, baking soda, and salt. Add the chives and peppers and blend well. In a small bowl, whisk together the egg whites and milk until well mixed. Stir the liquid ingredients into the dry ingredients just until the dry are moistened, about 10 strokes.

Spoon the batter into the pan and sprinkle with the remaining 1 tablespoon cornmeal. Bake for 30 to 35 minutes, or until golden brown and a wooden skewer inserted in the center of the loaf comes out clean.

Cool for 10 minutes in the baking pan. Remove from the pan and serve warm or transfer to a wire rack to cool completely.

MAKES 12 SLICES
Per slice: 68 cal., less than 1.0 g. fat, 1.5 g. fiber

Granola-Banana Bread

This bread is better tasting—and better for you—than cake or short-bread cookies. Toast it and lightly spread with low-fat cream cheese.

2 cups whole wheat flour	1 cup plus 2 tablespoons
1 cup brown sugar	fat-free granola
2 teaspoons baking soda	2 cups nonfat buttermilk
$\frac{1}{2}$ teaspoon salt	1 medium-ripe banana,
1 teaspoon ground cinnamon	mashed

Preheat the oven to 375° F. Lightly coat a 9 × 5 × 2½ inch loaf pan with nonstick cooking spray.

In a large bowl, sift together the flour, sugar, baking soda, salt, and cinnamon. Add the granola and stir to incorporate thoroughly. In a small bowl, whisk together the buttermilk and banana until well mixed. Stir the liquid ingredients into the dry ingredients just until the dry are moistened, about 10 strokes.

Spoon the batter into the loaf pan and bake for 30 to 40 minutes, or until golden brown and a wooden skewer inserted in the center of the loaf comes out clean.

Cool for 10 minutes in the baking pan. Remove from the pan and serve warm or transfer to a wire rack to cool completely.

MAKES 12 SLICES
Per slice: 201 cal., less than 1.0 g. fat, 4.6 g. fiber

Sweet Fennel Bread

Chopped apple provides moistness, and apple and brown sugar add sweetness to this fennel bread. Serve with a vegetable salad or a spicy gazpacho soup for lunch.

$\frac{1}{2}$ cup pitted dates
$\frac{1}{2}$ cup currants or raisins
2 cups apple cider
$1\frac{1}{2}$ teaspoons fennel seeds
$\frac{1}{2}$ cup cornmeal
$1\frac{1}{2}$ cups all-purpose flour
2 teaspoons baking powder
$\frac{1}{2}$ teaspoon baking soda

$\frac{1}{2}$ teaspoon salt
1 teaspoon ground cinnamon
1 cup peeled chopped tart apples, such as Granny Smith
2 large egg whites, lightly beaten
$\frac{1}{2}$ cup dark brown sugar

Preheat the oven to 375° F. Lightly coat a 9 × 5 × 2½ inch loaf pan with nonstick cooking spray.

Combine the dates, currants, apple cider, and fennel seeds in a medium saucepan. Bring to a boil over medium-high heat and simmer for 5 to 10 minutes, until liquid is reduced by half. Do not drain. Puree the mixture in a blender or food processor. Let cool to room temperature.

In a large bowl, sift together the cornmeal, flour, baking powder, baking soda, salt, and cinnamon. Add the apples and stir to incorporate thoroughly. In a small bowl, whisk together the egg whites, brown sugar, and date-currant puree until well mixed. Stir the liquid ingredients into the dry ingredients just until the dry are moistened, about 10 strokes.

Spoon the batter into the loaf pan and bake for 45 to 55 minutes, or until golden brown and a wooden skewer inserted in the center of the loaf comes out clean.

Cool for 10 minutes in the baking pan. Remove from the pan and serve warm or transfer to a wire rack to cool completely.

MAKES 12 SLICES
Per slice: 205 cal., less than 1.0 g. fat, 2.2 g. fiber

Scallion-Cumin Bread

Alongside Indian dishes or a spicy chili, this savory bread turns a meal into an ethnic feast.

1 cup all-purpose flour
1 cup whole wheat flour
2 teaspoons baking soda
1 teaspoon salt
1 teaspoon ground cumin
$\frac{1}{2}$ teaspoon freshly ground
   black pepper

1 cup thinly sliced scallions,
   white and green parts
1 cup nonfat plain yogurt
1 cup skim milk
$\frac{1}{4}$ cup molasses

Preheat the oven to 375° F. Lightly coat a 9 × 5 × 2½ inch loaf pan with nonstick cooking spray.

In a large bowl, sift together the flours, baking soda, salt, cumin, and pepper. Add the scallions and blend well. In a small bowl, whisk together the yogurt, milk, and molasses, then stir into the dry ingredients just until they are moistened, about 10 strokes. Spoon the batter into the pan and bake 50 to 60 minutes, or until golden brown and a skewer inserted in the center comes out clean.

Cool for 10 minutes in the baking pan. Remove from the pan and serve warm or transfer to a wire rack to cool completely.

MAKES 12 SLICES
Per slice: 108 cal., less than 1.0 g. fat, 1.7 g. fiber

Rosemary Honey Bread

An antipasto platter becomes something special with this bread in the center of the tray, ready to sop up any sauces. Serve toasted and cut into triangles.

2 cups whole wheat flour	2 teaspoons salt
1 cup all-purpose flour	3 tablespoons fresh or dried
1/2 cup cornmeal	rosemary leaves, chopped
1 teaspoon baking powder	1 cup honey
2 teaspoons baking soda	2 cups nonfat plain yogurt

Preheat the oven to 375° F. Lightly coat a 9-inch cast-iron skillet or a 10 × 15 inch baking sheet with nonstick cooking spray.

In a large bowl, sift together the whole wheat and all-purpose flours, cornmeal, baking powder, baking soda, and salt. Add the rosemary, honey, and yogurt and stir together to make a firm dough, about 15 strokes. Add more yogurt if necessary; the dough should be fairly wet. Moisten your hands and knead the dough gently on a floured work surface for about 3 minutes, until the dough is smooth and uniform in consistency. Put the dough into the skillet to fit. Or shape the dough into a round loaf, place on the baking sheet, and cut a 1/2-inch-deep × across the top, using a sharp knife. Bake for 35 to 45 minutes, or until the loaf is nicely browned and has a hollow sound when tapped on the bottom.

Cool for 10 minutes in the skillet or on the baking sheet. Remove from the pan and serve warm or transfer to a wire rack to cool completely.

MAKES 12 SLICES
Per slice: 232 cal., less than 1.0 g. fat, 3.3 g. fiber

Savory Breads

Anise-Raisin-Walnut Bread

Anise complements the intense flavors of some of the stronger cheeses, such as goat cheese. Sliced thin and toasted, it also works well with Eggplant Jelly (see page 90).

1 cup dark raisins	1 teaspoon salt
1 cup hot water	2 teaspoons anise seed
$\frac{1}{4}$ cup honey	$\frac{1}{4}$ cup plus 1 tablespoon
1 tablespoon baking soda	chopped walnuts
1 cup all-purpose flour	3 tablespoons vegetable oil
1 cup whole wheat flour	

Combine the raisins, water, and honey in a large bowl and stir in the baking soda. Cover and let sit for 1 hour.

Preheat the oven to 375° F. Lightly coat a 9 × 5 × 2½ inch loaf pan with nonstick cooking spray.

In a large bowl, sift together the all-purpose and whole wheat flours and salt. Add the anise seeds and ¼ cup of the walnuts and stir to incorporate thoroughly. Uncover the raisins, add the oil, and stir to blend. Add the raisin mixture to the dry ingredients and stir just until the dry are moistened, about 15 strokes. The batter should be thick.

Spoon the batter into the loaf pan and sprinkle with the remaining 1 tablespoon of walnuts. Bake for 50 to 60 minutes, or until light golden brown and a wooden skewer inserted in the center of the loaf comes out clean.

Cool for 10 minutes in the baking pan. Remove from the pan and serve warm or transfer to a wire rack to cool completely.

MAKES 12 SLICES
Per slice: 178 cal. (25% from fat), 5.2 g. fat, 2.1 g. fiber

Buckwheat-Sage Bread

Layer sliced tomatoes seasoned with cracked pepper and extra virgin olive oil on a thick slice of this robust bread, and it can be a nice lunch.

3/4 cup buckwheat flour
3/4 cup whole wheat flour
2 teaspoons baking powder
1/2 teaspoon salt
1/2 teaspoon freshly ground black pepper
1/2 cup currants
1/2 cup finely chopped onion

1 tablespoon finely chopped fresh sage leaves or 2 teaspoons finely chopped dried sage leaves
1 large egg, lightly beaten
1 cup skim milk
2 tablespoons olive oil

Preheat the oven to 375° F. Lightly coat a 9 × 5 × 2½ inch loaf pan with nonstick cooking spray.

In a large bowl, sift together the buckwheat and whole wheat flours, baking powder, salt, and pepper. Add the currants, onions, and sage and stir to incorporate thoroughly. In a small bowl, whisk together the egg, milk, and oil until well mixed. Stir the liquid ingredients into the dry ingredients just until the dry are moistened, about 10 strokes.

Spoon the batter into the loaf pan and bake for 45 to 55 minutes, or until light golden brown and a wooden skewer inserted in the center of the loaf comes out clean.

Cool for 10 minutes in the baking pan. Remove from the pan and serve warm or transfer to a wire rack to cool completely.

MAKES 12 SLICES
Per slice: 98 cal. (27% from fat), 3.0 g. fat, 1.9 g. fiber

Currant-Thyme Bread

Light in color and delicately spiced, this bread gets a flavor boost from white pepper and fresh thyme. A treat on its own, it also goes wonderfully with all sorts of meals. Serve it with mushroom soup or grilled fish.

1 cup currants
$^{1}/_{2}$ cup hot water
$^{2}/_{3}$ cup all-purpose flour
$^{2}/_{3}$ cup whole wheat flour
2 teaspoons baking powder
$^{1}/_{2}$ teaspoon baking soda
$^{1}/_{2}$ teaspoon salt
$^{1}/_{2}$ teaspoon freshly ground white pepper
$^{1}/_{2}$ teaspoon ground ginger
$^{1}/_{2}$ teaspoon ground allspice

4 large egg whites, lightly beaten
3 tablespoons canola oil or melted unsalted butter
1 cup low-fat plain yogurt
2 tablespoons fresh thyme leaves or 2 teaspoons dried thyme leaves
Thyme sprigs for garnish (optional)

Preheat the oven to 375° F. Lightly coat a 9 × 5 × 2½ inch loaf pan with nonstick cooking spray.

In a small saucepan, combine the currants and hot water and bring them to a simmer over medium heat. Let simmer for 15 minutes, until the currants have plumped up. Remove from the heat and drain.

In a large bowl, sift together the all-purpose and whole wheat flours, baking powder, baking soda, salt, pepper, ginger, and allspice. In a small bowl, whisk together the egg whites, oil, yogurt, and thyme until well mixed. Stir the liquid ingredients into the dry ingredients just until the dry are moistened, about 10 strokes. Gently fold in the currants.

Spoon the batter into the loaf pan and, if desired, arrange thyme sprigs on top of the bread. Bake for 45 to 55 minutes, or until light golden brown and a wooden skewer inserted in the center of the loaf comes out clean.

Cool for 10 minutes in the baking pan. Remove from the pan and serve warm or transfer to a wire rack to cool completely.

MAKES 12 SLICES
Per slice: 121 cal. (26% from fat), 3.6 g. fat, 1.8 g. fiber

Fresh Herb Bread

With a gardenful of fresh herbs, this tasty bread also makes a wonderful stuffing for turkey or chicken.

$^1/_2$ cup all-purpose flour
1 cup whole wheat flour
2 teaspoons baking powder
$^1/_2$ teaspoon baking soda
$^1/_2$ teaspoon salt
$^1/_2$ teaspoon freshly ground
   black pepper
$^1/_2$ cup plus 1 tablespoon
   quick rolled oats
2 tablespoons chopped fresh
   parsley

2 tablespoons chopped fresh
   mint leaves
2 tablespoons chopped fresh
   sage leaves
2 tablespoons chopped fresh
   chives
2 large eggs, lightly beaten
1 cup low-fat buttermilk
1 tablespoon olive oil

Preheat the oven to 375° F. Lightly coat a 9 × 5 × 2$^1/_2$ inch loaf pan with nonstick cooking spray.

In a large bowl, sift together the flours, baking powder, baking soda, salt, and pepper. Add $^1/_2$ cup of the oats, the parsley, mint, sage, and chives and blend well. In a small bowl, whisk together the eggs, buttermilk, and oil until well mixed and stir into the dry ingredients just until they are moistened, about 10 strokes.

Spoon the batter into the pan. Sprinkle the top with the remaining tablespoon of oats. Bake 45 to 55 minutes, or until light brown and a skewer inserted in the center comes out clean.

Cool for 10 minutes in the baking pan. Remove from the pan and serve warm or transfer to a wire rack to cool completely.

MAKES 12 SLICES
Per slice: 95 cal. (27% from fat), 2.9 g. fat, 1.7 g. fiber

Garlic-Scallion Bread

The intense garlic and scallion flavors in this bread lend themselves nicely to smoked fishes, especially salmon. For added indulgence, spread with a low-fat cream cheese. You may never want bagels again.

³⁄₄ cup whole wheat flour
³⁄₄ cup all-purpose flour
¹⁄₂ cup yellow cornmeal
1 tablespoon baking powder
¹⁄₂ teaspoon salt
¹⁄₂ teaspoon freshly ground white pepper

1 large egg, lightly beaten
3 tablespoons olive oil
1 cup skim milk
1 tablespoon minced garlic
1 cup plus 2 tablespoons thinly sliced scallions, green and white parts

Preheat the oven to 375° F. Lightly coat a 9 × 5 × 2½ inch loaf pan with nonstick cooking spray.

In a large bowl, sift together the whole wheat and all-purpose flours, cornmeal, baking powder, salt, and pepper. In a small bowl, whisk together the egg, oil, milk, and garlic. Stir the liquid ingredients into the dry ingredients just until the dry are moistened, about 10 strokes. Gently fold in 1 cup of the scallions.

Spoon the batter into the loaf pan and sprinkle the remaining 2 tablespoons scallions evenly on top of the bread. Bake for 45 to 55 minutes, or until light golden brown and a wooden skewer inserted in the center of the loaf comes out clean.

Cool for 10 minutes in the baking pan. Remove from the pan and serve warm or transfer to a wire rack to cool completely.

MAKES 12 SLICES
Per slice: 123 cal. (30% from fat), 4.1 g. fat, 1.6 g. fiber

Jalapeño Corn Bread

For a less spicy version, reduce the amount of pepper or replace it with two tablespoons of freshly snipped chives. When the bread is baked in an 8-inch square baking pan (for 30 to 40 minutes), everyone gets more golden crust.

1 cup all-purpose flour	3 tablespoons olive oil
1 cup plus 1 tablespoon yellow cornmeal	$\frac{1}{2}$ cup nonfat sour cream
3 teaspoons baking powder	2 tablespoons jalapeño peppers, seeded and finely chopped
1 teaspoon salt	
2 large eggs, lightly beaten	1 cup fresh or frozen and thawed corn kernels
1 cup water	

Preheat the oven to 375° F. Lightly coat a 9 × 5 × 2½ inch loaf pan with nonstick cooking spray.

In a large bowl, sift together the flour, 1 cup of the cornmeal, baking powder, and salt. In a small bowl, whisk together the eggs, water, olive oil, sour cream, and jalapeño peppers until well mixed. Add the liquid ingredients to the dry ingredients and stir just until the dry are moistened, about 10 strokes. Gently fold in the corn.

Spoon the batter into the loaf pan and sprinkle with the remaining 1 tablespoon of cornmeal. Bake for 45 to 55 minutes, or until light golden brown and a wooden skewer inserted in the center of the loaf comes out clean.

Cool for 10 minutes in the baking pan. Remove from the pan and serve warm or transfer to a wire rack to cool completely.

MAKES 12 SLICES
Per slice: 166 cal. (25% from fat), 4.5 g. fat, 1.4 g. fiber

Lemon-Pepper Bread

Tart yogurt, fresh lemon, and spicy pepper give this bread a kick. Try it with Apple Preserve (see page 88).

$1/2$ cup whole wheat flour
$1/2$ cup all-purpose flour
1 cup white cornmeal
$1^1/2$ teaspoons baking powder
$1/2$ teaspoon baking soda
1 teaspoon salt
1 tablespoon freshly ground black pepper
1 large egg, lightly beaten
2 tablespoons olive oil

1 cup nonfat plain yogurt
$1/4$ cup fresh lemon juice
2 tablespoons grated lemon zest

Lemon-Pepper Glaze

3 tablespoons fresh lemon juice
$1/2$ teaspoon hot chili sauce
1 teaspoon olive oil

Preheat the oven to 375° F. Lightly coat a 9 × 5 × $2^1/2$ inch loaf pan with nonstick cooking spray.

In a large bowl, sift together the flours, cornmeal, baking powder, baking soda, salt, and pepper. In a small bowl, whisk together the egg, oil, yogurt, lemon juice, and zest and stir into the dry ingredients just until they are moistened, about 10 strokes.

Spoon the batter into the pan and bake 45 to 55 minutes, or until golden brown and a skewer inserted in the center comes out clean.

To make the glaze, combine the lemon juice, chili sauce, and olive oil. When the bread is done, brush the warm top with the glaze. Cool for 10 minutes in the baking pan. Remove from the pan and serve warm or cool on a wire rack.

MAKES 12 SLICES
Per slice: 107 cal. (26% from fat), 3.2 g. fat, 1.6 g. fiber

Cracked Wheat—Rye Bread

Bulgur distinguishes this quick bread from other, traditional ryes. Try eating it with Apricot-Lemon Spread (see page 88), with a salad for lunch.

$^1/_2$ cup whole wheat flour
1 cup rye flour
1 tablespoon baking powder
$^1/_2$ teaspoon salt
$^1/_4$ cup bulgur
$^1/_2$ teaspoon crushed fennel
   seeds
$^1/_2$ teaspoon crushed caraway
   seeds
1 large egg, lightly beaten
1 cup water
2 tablespoons olive oil

Preheat the oven to 375° F. Lightly coat a 9 × 5 × 2$^1/_2$ inch loaf pan with nonstick cooking spray.

In a large bowl, sift together the whole wheat and rye flours, baking powder, and salt. Add the bulgur, fennel and caraway seeds, and stir to incorporate thoroughly. In a small bowl, whisk together the egg, water, and oil until well mixed. Stir the liquid ingredients into the dry ingredients just until the dry are moistened, about 10 strokes.

Spoon the batter into the loaf pan and bake for 45 to 55 minutes, or until golden brown and a wooden skewer inserted in the center of the loaf comes out clean.

Cool for 10 minutes in the baking pan. Remove from the pan and serve warm or transfer to a wire rack to cool completely.

MAKES 12 SLICES
Per slice: 89 cal. (29% from fat), 3.0 g. fat, 2.4 g. fiber

Onion-Dill Bread

To make the most of this bread, slather it with low-fat cottage cheese or a sun-dried tomato and herb spread.

1 cup yellow cornmeal
$^1/_2$ cup whole wheat flour
2 teaspoons baking powder
$^1/_2$ teaspoon baking soda
1 teaspoon salt
$^1/_4$ teaspoon freshly ground
   white pepper
1 large egg, lightly beaten
2 tablespoons olive oil

$^1/_2$ cup nonfat plain yogurt
$^1/_2$ cup skim milk
$^1/_2$ cup plus 1 tablespoon
   finely chopped onions
$^1/_4$ cup plus 1 tablespoon
   chopped fresh dill or 2
   tablespoons plus 1
   teaspoon dried dill weed

Preheat the oven to 375° F. Lightly coat a 9 × 5 × 2$^1/_2$ inch loaf pan with nonstick cooking spray.

In a large bowl, sift together the cornmeal, flour, baking powder, baking soda, salt, and pepper. In a small bowl, whisk together the egg, oil, yogurt, milk, $^1/_2$ cup onions, and $^1/_4$ cup fresh or 2 tablespoons dried dill until well mixed and stir into the dry ingredients just until they are moistened, about 10 strokes.

Spoon the batter into the loaf pan and sprinkle with the remaining 1 tablespoon onions and 1 tablespoon fresh or 1 teaspoon dried dill. Bake for 45 to 55 minutes, or until light golden brown and a wooden skewer inserted in the center of the loaf comes out clean.

Cool for 10 minutes in the baking pan. Remove from the pan and serve warm or transfer to a wire rack to cool completely.

MAKES 12 SLICES
Per slice: 104 cal. (26% from fat), 2.9 g. fat, 1.2 g. fiber

Potato-Poppy Bread

Potatoes add a wonderful, smooth texture to this bread. Try it lightly toasted with Mango Chutney (see page 90), as a starter for dinner.

2 cups all-purpose flour
1 tablespoon baking powder
1 teaspoon salt
$1/2$ teaspoon freshly ground
   white pepper
$1/2$ teaspoon caraway seeds
2 large eggs, lightly beaten
3 tablespoons unsalted
   butter, melted

1 cup skim milk
1 cup coarsely mashed
   cooked potatoes
1 tablespoon freshly grated
   Parmesan cheese
2 teaspoons poppy seeds

Preheat the oven to 375° F. Lightly coat a 9 × 5 × 2½ inch loaf pan with nonstick cooking spray.

In a large bowl, sift together the flour, baking powder, salt, and pepper. Add the caraway seeds and stir to incorporate thoroughly. In a small bowl, whisk together the eggs, butter, milk, and potatoes until well mixed. Stir the liquid ingredients into the dry ingredients just until the dry are moistened, about 10 strokes.

Spoon the batter into the loaf pan and sprinkle the cheese and poppy seeds evenly over the top. Bake for 45 to 55 minutes, or until light golden brown and a wooden skewer inserted in the center of the loaf comes out clean.

Cool for 10 minutes in the baking pan. Remove from the pan and serve warm or transfer to a wire rack to cool completely.

MAKES 12 SLICES
Per slice: 127 cal. (25% from fat), 3.4 g. fat, 0.9 g. fiber

Sugar and Spice Bread

While savory spices combined with sweet maple syrup might sound strange, the result is terrific. Serve it for hors d'oeuvres, topped with a mild low-fat cheese and olive tapenade.

$^1/_2$ cup whole wheat flour
1 cup all-purpose flour
$^1/_2$ cup yellow cornmeal
2 teaspoons baking powder
$^1/_2$ teaspoon baking soda
$^3/_4$ teaspoon salt
$^1/_8$ teaspoon cayenne pepper
$^1/_2$ teaspoon crushed fennel seeds
$^1/_2$ teaspoon ground cumin
$^1/_2$ teaspoon ground ginger

2 large eggs, lightly beaten
$^1/_4$ cup vegetable oil
1 cup pure maple syrup
$^1/_2$ cup skim milk

Sweet Fennel Topping

1 teaspoon crushed fennel seeds
1 teaspoon sugar
Pinch of cayenne pepper

Preheat the oven to 375° F. Lightly coat a 9 × 5 × 2½ inch loaf pan with nonstick cooking spray.

In a large bowl, sift together the whole wheat and all-purpose flours, cornmeal, baking powder, baking soda, salt, pepper, fennel, cumin, and ginger. In a small bowl, whisk together the eggs, oil, syrup, and milk, then stir into the dry ingredients just until they are moistened, about 10 strokes. Spoon the batter into the pan.

For the topping, mix together the fennel, sugar, and cayenne and sprinkle over the bread. Bake 45 to 55 minutes, or until golden brown and a skewer inserted in the center comes out clean. Cool for 10 minutes in the pan. Serve warm or cool on a wire rack.

MAKES 12 SLICES
Per slice: 197 cal. (26% from fat), 5.8 g. fat, 1.3 g. fiber

Tomato-Herb Bread

Tomato puree and fresh tomatoes make this herb bread a favorite. It's best served with seafood or dunked in a robust clam chowder.

$1/2$ cup yellow cornmeal
$1^1/2$ cups all-purpose flour
2 teaspoons baking powder
$1/2$ teaspoon baking soda
$1/2$ teaspoon salt
$1/4$ teaspoon freshly ground black pepper
1 large egg, lightly beaten
2 tablespoons olive oil
$1/2$ cup seeded and finely chopped fresh tomatoes

1 cup tomato puree
$1/4$ cup thinly sliced scallions, green and white parts
1 teaspoon fresh or dried oregano leaves
1 tablespoon chopped fresh dill or 1 teaspoon dried dill weed
1 tablespoon chopped fresh cilantro

Preheat the oven to 375° F. Lightly coat a 9 × 5 × 2½ inch loaf pan with nonstick cooking spray.

In a large bowl, sift together the cornmeal, all-purpose flour, baking powder, baking soda, salt, and pepper. In a small bowl, whisk together the egg, oil, chopped tomatoes, tomato puree, scallions, oregano, dill, and cilantro until well mixed and stir into the dry ingredients just until they are moistened, about 10 strokes.

Spoon the batter into the loaf pan and bake for 45 to 55 minutes, or until lightly browned and a wooden skewer inserted in the center of the loaf comes out clean.

Cool for 10 minutes in the baking pan. Remove from the pan and serve warm or transfer to a wire rack to cool completely.

MAKES 12 SLICES
Per slice: 107 cal. (25% from fat), 3.0 g. fat, 1.4 g. fiber

Dessert Breads

Cherry-Almond Bread

Never again will you crave fat-laden Danish or strudel when this bread, thinly sliced and warm, is on hand. Serve with the summer's best strawberries or blueberries.

2 cups dried cherries
1 cup hot water
2 cups all-purpose flour
$1/2$ cup sugar
2 teaspoons baking powder
$1/2$ teaspoon baking soda
$1/2$ teaspoon salt
$1/4$ teaspoon ground nutmeg
1 large egg, lightly beaten

1 large egg white, lightly beaten
$1/2$ cup fresh orange juice
$3/4$ cup skim milk
3 tablespoons unsalted butter, melted
2 tablespoons chopped almonds

Preheat the oven to 375° F. Lightly coat a 9 × 5 × 2½ inch loaf pan with nonstick cooking spray.

In a small bowl, combine the cherries and hot water. Let them stand for 10 minutes, then drain well.

In a large bowl, sift together the flour, sugar, baking powder, baking soda, salt, and nutmeg. Add the cherries and blend well. In a small bowl, whisk together the egg, egg white, orange juice, milk, and butter until well mixed. Stir the liquid ingredients into the dry ingredients just until the dry are moistened, about 10 strokes. Spoon the batter into the pan and sprinkle with the almonds. Bake 40 to 50 minutes, or until golden brown and a skewer inserted in the center comes out clean. Cool for 10 minutes in the pan. Remove from the pan and serve warm or cool on a wire rack.

MAKES 12 SLICES
Per slice: 226 cal. (15% from fat), 4.3 g. fat, 2.2 g. fiber

Fresh Peach Bread

Fresh mint leaves add great flavor to this bread. Serve it warm, topped with nonfat vanilla ice cream and fresh berries.

1½ cups all-purpose flour
½ cup sugar
3 teaspoons baking powder
½ teaspoon salt
4 teaspoons chopped fresh mint leaves
1 tablespoon grated lemon zest
2 large eggs, lightly beaten

1 cup nonfat buttermilk
3 tablespoons unsalted butter, melted
1 cup peeled chopped peaches
½ cup peeled thinly sliced peaches
2 teaspoons brown sugar

Preheat the oven to 375° F. Lightly coat a 9 × 5 × 2½ inch loaf pan with nonstick cooking spray.

In a large bowl, sift together the flour, sugar, baking powder, and salt. Add 3 teaspoons of the mint and the lemon zest and stir to incorporate thoroughly. In a small bowl, whisk together the eggs, buttermilk, and butter until well mixed. Stir the liquid ingredients into the dry ingredients just until the dry are moistened, about 10 strokes. Gently fold in the 1 cup chopped peaches. Spoon the batter into the loaf pan. Arrange the peach slices and remaining mint on top of the batter and sprinkle with the brown sugar. Bake for 40 to 50 minutes, or until golden brown and a wooden skewer inserted in the center of the loaf comes out clean.

Cool for 10 minutes in the baking pan. Remove from the pan and serve warm or transfer to a wire rack to cool completely.

MAKES 12 SLICES
Per slice: 146 cal. (25% from fat), 4.0 g. fat, 1.3 g. fiber

Old-Fashioned Gingerbread

Grandmother's recipe is adapted with whole wheat flour to make a dark glossy bread. Serve warm with nonfat vanilla ice cream or toasted with jam. This bread keeps well for up to one week in the refrigerator.

1 cup whole wheat flour	2 large eggs, lightly beaten
1 cup all-purpose flour	$\frac{1}{2}$ cup molasses
1 teaspoon baking soda	$\frac{1}{2}$ cup brown sugar
$\frac{1}{2}$ teaspoon salt	1 cup water
$2\frac{1}{2}$ teaspoons ground ginger	1 teaspoon grated orange zest
1 teaspoon ground cinnamon	4 tablespoons unsalted
$\frac{1}{2}$ teaspoon ground nutmeg	butter, melted
$\frac{1}{2}$ teaspoon ground allspice	

Preheat the oven to 375° F. Lightly coat a 9 × 5 × 2½ inch loaf pan with nonstick cooking spray.

In a large bowl, sift together the whole wheat and all-purpose flours, baking soda, salt, ginger, cinnamon, nutmeg, and allspice. In a small bowl, whisk together the eggs, molasses, brown sugar, water, orange zest, and butter until well mixed. Stir the liquid ingredients into the dry ingredients just until the dry are moistened, about 10 strokes. Spoon the batter into the loaf pan and bake for 40 to 50 minutes, or until golden brown and a wooden skewer inserted in the center of the loaf comes out clean.

Cool for 10 minutes in the baking pan. Remove from the pan and serve warm or transfer to a wire rack to cool completely.

MAKES 12 SLICES
Per slice: 175 cal. (25% from fat), 4.9 g. fat, 1.6 g. fiber

Honey-Glaze Tea Bread

With a cup of tea as one of its ten ingredients, this simple recipe makes a deceptively elegant treat. For a sweeter dessert, top with nonfat ice cream and drizzle with your favorite honey.

2 cups all-purpose flour
2 teaspoons baking powder
$\frac{1}{2}$ teaspoon salt
1 teaspoon ground cinnamon
2 large eggs, lightly beaten
1 cup sugar
$\frac{1}{4}$ cup corn oil

1 cup strong tea, at room
   temperature

Honey Glaze

3 tablespoons honey
2 tablespoons fresh lemon
   juice

Preheat the oven to 375° F. Lightly coat a 9 × 5 × 2½ inch loaf pan with nonstick cooking spray.

In a large bowl, sift together the flour, baking powder, salt, and cinnamon. In another large bowl, whisk together the eggs, sugar, oil, and tea until well mixed. While whisking, slowly add the dry to the liquid ingredients. Continue whisking just until incorporated, about 10 strokes. Spoon the batter into the loaf pan and bake for 50 to 60 minutes, or until golden brown and a wooden skewer inserted in the center of the loaf comes out clean.

While the bread is baking, make the glaze. Combine the honey and lemon juice in a small pan and warm over medium heat. When the bread is done and still warm, brush the top with the glaze, until all is used.

Cool for 10 minutes in the baking pan. Remove from the pan and serve warm or transfer to a wire rack to cool completely.

MAKES 12 SLICES
Per slice: 203 cal. (24% from fat), 5.5 g. fat, 2.6 g. fiber

Indian Pumpkin Bread

Make this autumnal bread with fresh pumpkin before the frost sets in. Serve toasted with a warm apple or pear compote.

$\frac{1}{2}$ cup all-purpose flour
1 cup cornmeal
1 teaspoon baking powder
1 teaspoon baking soda
$\frac{1}{2}$ teaspoon salt
$\frac{1}{2}$ teaspoon ground nutmeg
1 teaspoon ground cinnamon
$\frac{1}{2}$ cup grated pumpkin
$\frac{1}{2}$ cup golden raisins

2 large eggs, lightly beaten
$\frac{1}{2}$ cup brown sugar
$\frac{1}{2}$ cup skim milk
1 cup fresh or canned
   pumpkin puree
3 tablespoons unsalted
   butter, melted
2 tablespoons pumpkin seeds

Preheat the oven to 375° F. Lightly coat a 9 × 5 × 2½ inch loaf pan with nonstick cooking spray.

In a large bowl, sift together the flour, cornmeal, baking powder, baking soda, salt, nutmeg, and cinnamon. Add the grated pumpkin and raisins and stir to incorporate thoroughly. In a small bowl, whisk together the eggs, brown sugar, milk, pumpkin puree, and butter until well mixed. Stir the liquid ingredients into the dry ingredients just until the dry are moistened, about 10 strokes. Spoon the batter into the loaf pan and sprinkle with the pumpkin seeds. Bake for 45 to 50 minutes, or until golden brown and a wooden skewer inserted in the center of the loaf comes out clean.

Cool for 10 minutes in the baking pan. Remove from the pan and serve warm or transfer to a wire rack to cool completely.

MAKES 12 SLICES
Per slice: 156 cal. (27% from fat), 4.9 g. fat, 1.9 g. fiber

Lemon–Poppy Seed Bread

The traditional tea-time treat is updated and lower in fat when made with yogurt. Lemon juice and zest provide the strong citrus flavor.

2 cups cake flour
2 teaspoons baking powder
1 teaspoon baking soda
$\frac{1}{4}$ teaspoon salt
$\frac{1}{4}$ cup poppy seeds
2 large eggs, lightly beaten
$\frac{3}{4}$ cup sugar
1 cup plain, nonfat yogurt
$\frac{1}{2}$ cup fresh lemon juice

2 tablespoons grated lemon zest
3 tablespoons unsalted butter, melted

Lemon Glaze

$\frac{1}{3}$ cup fresh lemon juice
$\frac{1}{3}$ cup sugar

Preheat the oven to 375° F. Lightly coat a 9 × 5 × 2½ inch loaf pan with nonstick cooking spray.

In a large bowl, sift together the flour, baking powder, baking soda, and salt. Add the poppy seeds and blend well. In a small bowl, whisk together the eggs, sugar, yogurt, lemon juice, zest, and butter until well mixed and stir into the dry ingredients just until they are moistened, about 10 strokes. Spoon the batter into the pan. Bake 40 to 50 minutes, or until golden brown and a skewer inserted in the center comes out clean.

To make the glaze, combine the lemon juice and sugar in a small pan. Bring to a boil over medium heat and stir until the sugar dissolves. Brush the warm bread with the glaze until all is used.

Cool for 10 minutes in the baking pan. Remove from the pan and serve warm or transfer to a wire rack to cool completely.

MAKES 12 SLICES
Per slice: 184 cal. (25% from fat), 5.2 g. fat, 1.1 g. fiber

Pear-Cardamom Bread

If it's available, use fresh cardamom and grind the seeds yourself. The difference between preground and fresh is vast. Drizzle with maple syrup or honey or serve with frozen yogurt.

1 cup all-purpose flour
1 cup cornmeal
2 teaspoons baking powder
1 teaspoon baking soda
$1/2$ teaspoon salt
2 teaspoons ground
   cardamom
1 large egg, lightly beaten
2 large egg whites, lightly
   beaten
$1/2$ cup light brown sugar
1 cup unsweetened
   applesauce

1 tablespoon grated lemon
   zest
4 tablespoons canola oil
2 cups peeled chopped pears

Cardamom-Sugar Topping

2 tablespoons light brown
   sugar
2 tablespoons all-purpose
   flour
$1/4$ teaspoon ground
   cardamom
1 tablespoon canola oil

Preheat the oven to 375° F. Lightly coat a 9 × 5 × 2½ inch loaf pan with nonstick cooking spray.

In a large bowl, sift together the flour, cornmeal, baking powder, baking soda, salt, and cardamom. In a small bowl, whisk together the egg, egg whites, brown sugar, applesauce, zest, and oil until well mixed. Stir the liquid ingredients into the dry ingredients just until the dry are moistened, about 10 strokes. Gently fold in the chopped pears. Spoon the batter into the loaf pan.

To make the topping, mix the brown sugar, flour, and cardamom together. Add the oil and stir until crumbly. Sprinkle over the bread and pat gently. Bake 40 to 50 minutes, or until golden brown and a skewer inserted in the center of the loaf comes out clean. Cool for 10 minutes in the baking pan. Remove from the pan and serve warm or cool on a wire rack.

MAKES 12 SLICES
Per slice: 185 cal. (26% from fat), 5.5 g. fat, 2.0 g. fiber

Plum Pudding Bread

This bread is more similar in texture and consistency to an English pudding than a bread. Serve with nonfat frozen ice cream.

1 cup all-purpose flour	$\frac{1}{2}$ cup plus 1 tablespoon
$\frac{1}{2}$ teaspoon salt	sugar
2 large eggs, lightly beaten	1 cup skim milk
2 large egg whites, lightly	2 cups thinly sliced ripe red
beaten	plums

Preheat the oven to 400° F. Lightly coat an 8-inch or 9-inch flan dish or ceramic tart pan with nonstick cooking spray.

In a small bowl, sift together the flour and salt. In a large bowl, whisk together the eggs, egg whites, and $\frac{1}{2}$ cup sugar until well mixed. Add the flour mixture and milk to the egg mixture and whisk until the batter is creamy and smooth.

Arrange half of the plums on the bottom of the flan dish or pan and pour the batter on top. Arrange the remaining plums on top and sprinkle with the remaining 1 tablespoon of sugar.

Bake for 30 to 40 minutes, or until golden brown. The dessert will rise during baking and fall when taken out of the oven.

Serve warm directly from the pan.

MAKES 12 SERVINGS
Per slice: 105 cal. (10% from fat), 1.1 g. fat, 0.8 g. fiber

Sweet Rhubarb Bread

Rhubarb is most often served as a fruit rather than a vegetable, baked into pies, crumbles, crisps, and breads. Avoid the leaves, however; they are poisonous.

2 cups all-purpose flour
1 tablespoon baking powder
1/2 teaspoon salt
1/2 teaspoon ground
   cinnamon
1 large egg, lightly beaten
1 cup sugar
1 cup skim milk
4 tablespoons unsalted
   butter, melted

1 cup 1/2-inch diced fresh
   rhubarb

Lemon-Almond Topping

1 tablespoon grated lemon
   zest
1/4 teaspoon ground
   cinnamon
2 tablespoons finely chopped
   almonds

Preheat the oven to 375° F. Lightly coat a 9 × 5 × 2½ inch loaf pan with nonstick cooking spray.

In a large bowl, sift together the flour, baking powder, salt, and cinnamon. In a small bowl, whisk together the egg, sugar, milk, and butter until well mixed, and stir into the dry ingredients just until they are moistened, about 10 strokes. Gently fold in the rhubarb and spoon the batter into the pan. For the topping, mix together the lemon zest, cinnamon, and almonds and sprinkle on the batter.

Bake 45 to 50 minutes, or until golden brown and a wooden skewer inserted in the center comes out clean. Cool for 10 minutes in the pan. Remove from the pan and serve warm or cool on a wire rack.

MAKES 12 SLICES
Per slice: 191 cal. (24% from fat), 5.2 g. fat, 0.9 g. fiber

Maple Nut–Spice Bread

Black pepper intensifies the other spices in this bread to create a delicious dessert. Make it two days in advance for the best results.

2 cups all-purpose flour
2 teaspoons baking powder
¼ teaspoon salt
2 teaspoons freshly ground pepper
½ teaspoon ground cinnamon
½ teaspoon ground nutmeg
¼ teaspoon ground cloves

¼ teaspoon ground anise seeds
2 large eggs, lightly beaten
1 cup pure maple syrup
4 tablespoons unsalted butter, melted
1 tablespoon chopped pecans
1 tablespoon chopped walnuts

Preheat the oven to 375° F. Lightly coat a 9 × 5 × 2½ inch loaf pan with nonstick cooking spray.

In a large bowl, sift together the flour, baking powder, salt, pepper, cinnamon, nutmeg, cloves, and anise. In a small bowl, whisk together the eggs, maple syrup, and butter until well mixed. Stir the liquid ingredients into the dry ingredients just until the dry are moistened, about 10 strokes. Sprinkle with the chopped pecans and walnuts and bake for 40 to 50 minutes, or until golden brown and a wooden skewer inserted in the center of the loaf comes out clean.

Cool for 10 minutes in the baking pan. Remove from the pan and serve warm or transfer to a wire rack to cool completely.

For best results, wrap the bread in foil and let it sit at room temperature for 2 days before eating.

MAKES 12 SLICES
Per slice: 193 cal. (26% from fat), 5.6 g. fat, 0.8 g. fiber

Fresh Strawberry Bread

The best-tasting low-fat strawberry shortcake starts with a generous slice of this bread topped with fresh berries and their juices. Try it with a dollop of light whipped cream.

2 cups all-purpose flour
1 cup sugar
2 teaspoons baking powder
1 teaspoon baking soda
$\frac{1}{2}$ teaspoon salt
1 cup diced fresh strawberries
2 large eggs, lightly beaten
$\frac{1}{2}$ cup skim milk
$\frac{1}{2}$ cup frozen orange juice
   concentrate, thawed
3 tablespoons unsalted
   butter, melted

Strawberry-Coconut Glaze

3 tablespoons frozen orange
   juice concentrate, thawed
3 tablespoons all-fruit
   strawberry jam
1 tablespoon flaked unsweetened coconut
1 tablespoon unsalted butter,
   melted

Preheat the oven to 375° F. Lightly coat a 9 × 5 × 2½ inch loaf pan with nonstick cooking spray.

In a large bowl, sift together the flour, sugar, baking powder, baking soda, and salt. In a small bowl, lightly toss the strawberries with 1 tablespoon of the flour mixture until the strawberries are coated, and set aside. In another small bowl, whisk together the eggs, milk, orange juice concentrate, and butter until well mixed. Stir the liquid ingredients into the dry ingredients just until the dry are moistened, about 10 strokes. Gently fold in the strawberries and spoon the batter into the loaf pan. Bake for 40 to 50 minutes, or until golden brown and a wooden skewer inserted in the center of the loaf comes out clean.

To make the glaze, while the bread is baking, combine the orange juice concentrate, strawberry jam, coconut, and butter and mix well. When the bread is finished baking and still warm, brush it with the glaze until all is used.

Cool for 10 minutes in the baking pan. Remove from the pan and serve warm or transfer to a wire rack to cool completely.

MAKES 12 SLICES
Per slice: 222 cal. (20% from fat), 5.0 g. fat, 0.9 g. fiber

Orange-Chocolate Bread

Top this bread with caramelized fresh oranges or use as a base for orange trifle by layering with whipped cream and fruit.

2 cups all-purpose flour
1 cup sugar
2 teaspoons baking powder
1/2 teaspoon baking soda
3 teaspoons unsweetened
  dark cocoa powder
1/2 teaspoon salt
2 large eggs, lightly beaten
1/2 cup nonfat plain yogurt
1 cup frozen orange juice
  concentrate, thawed

1 tablespoon grated orange
  zest
3 tablespoons unsalted
  butter, melted
1 cup orange sections,
  chopped and drained
3 tablespoons chopped
  bittersweet chocolate

Preheat the oven to 375° F. Lightly coat a 9 × 5 × 2½ inch loaf pan with nonstick cooking spray.

In a large bowl, sift together the flour, sugar, baking powder, baking soda, cocoa powder, and salt. In a small bowl, whisk together the eggs, yogurt, orange juice concentrate, zest, and butter until well mixed and stir into the dry ingredients just until they are moistened, about 10 strokes. Gently fold in the orange sections. Spoon the batter into the pan and sprinkle with the chocolate. Bake for 40 to 50 minutes, or until golden brown and a skewer inserted in the center comes out clean.

Cool for 10 minutes in the baking pan. Remove from the pan and serve warm or transfer to a wire rack to cool completely.

MAKES 12 SLICES
Per slice: 246 cal. (21% from fat), 5.9 g. fat, 1.3 g. fiber

Spreads

Apple Preserve

Serve slightly warm as a topping over a scoop of nonfat ice cream as its own dessert, or spread on sweet and savory breads instead of jam. This preserve is also thick enough to make a nice filling for apple pie.

2 large firm apples, such as Cortland or Red Delicious, peeled, cored, and chopped
1/2 cup light brown sugar
1/4 cup apple cider or juice
1/2 cup fresh orange juice
1 tablespoon grated orange zest
1/4 teaspoon ground cardamom
1/4 teaspoon salt

Combine all of the ingredients in a medium saucepan and bring to a boil over medium heat, stirring frequently. Simmer for about 15 minutes, or until the mixture is reduced to 2 cups. Let cool completely. Transfer from the saucepan to a tightly covered container and refrigerate. The preserve will keep for about 4 weeks. Serve at room temperature or cold.

MAKES 2 CUPS
Per serving (1 tablespoon): 18 cal. (2% from fat), less than 1.0 g. fat

Apricot-Lemon Spread

This is a naturally sweet spread—no sugar added—that goes well with any of your favorite breakfast breads.

1 cup packed dried apricots
1/2 cup honey
Grated zest of 2 lemons
Juice of 2 lemons

Place the apricots in a bowl and cover with boiling water. Allow to stand at room temperature until softened, about 1 hour. Drain the apricots. In a food processor, combine the apricots, honey, lemon zest, and juice and puree until smooth. Transfer from the processor to a tightly covered container and refrigerate. The preserve will keep for about 8 weeks. Serve at room temperature or cold.

MAKES 1½ CUPS
Per serving (1 tablespoon): 35 cal. (1% from fat), less than 1.0 g. fat

Beet-Onion Preserve

Spread this sweet-and-sour preserve on any of the savory breads. It can also be served warm with a hearty bread such as High-Fiber Bread (see page 51).

1 cup peeled grated red beets	½ cup brown sugar
2 cups thinly sliced red onion	½ cup red wine vinegar

Combine the beets, onions, and brown sugar in a medium saucepan. Cook over medium-high heat, stirring, until the onions begin to brown and caramelize, about 30 minutes. Stir in the vinegar and bring to a boil. Cook over medium heat until all the liquid is evaporated, about 20 minutes. Let cool completely. Transfer from the saucepan to a tightly covered container and refrigerate. The preserve will keep for about 4 weeks. Serve at room temperature or cold.

MAKES 2½ CUPS
Per serving (1 tablespoon): 13 cal. (1% from fat), less than 1.0 g. fat

Eggplant Jelly

This unusual topping is completely fat-free and wonderful atop toasted slices of bread such as Sweet Potato Bread (see page 42) or Onion-Dill Bread (see page 69).

1 cup fresh orange juice
2 cups sugar
$\frac{1}{8}$ teaspoon ground anise
　seeds
$\frac{1}{2}$ teaspoon salt

2 medium eggplants, peeled, seeded, and chopped into $\frac{1}{2}$-inch cubes (about 2 cups)

Bring the orange juice and sugar to a boil over medium-high heat. Simmer for 2 minutes and add the anise, salt, and eggplant. Cook over medium-low heat until the eggplant is translucent, about 20 minutes. Cool completely. Transfer from the saucepan to a tightly covered container and refrigerate for up to 4 weeks. Serve at room temperature or cold.

MAKES 2$\frac{1}{2}$ CUPS
Per serving (1 tablespoon): 42 cal. (0% from fat), 0 g. fat

Mango Chutney

Toss out that old bottle of prepared sweet-and-sour sauce and replace it with this chutney. Slather it on warmed savory breads such as Potato-Poppy Bread (see page 70).

3 tablespoons minced garlic
3 tablespoons minced
　gingerroot

2 tablespoons vegetable oil
2 tablespoons dry mustard
2 teaspoons ground cumin

2 teaspoons chili powder

1 teaspoon freshly ground
black pepper

1 large Granny Smith apple,
peeled, cored, and chopped

2 cups chopped mango

1/2 cup red wine vinegar

1/2 cup sugar

2 tablespoons salt

In a large saucepan, over low heat, sweat the garlic and ginger in the oil for 5 minutes. Add the mustard, cumin, chili powder, and pepper and cook for 2 minutes. Add the apple, mango, vinegar, sugar, and salt and simmer until thick, about 30 minutes. Cool completely. Transfer to a tightly covered container and refrigerate for up to 4 weeks. Serve at room temperature.

MAKES 2 CUPS
Per serving (1 tablespoon): 34 cal. (28% from fat), 1.1 g. fat

Strawberry Jam

Everyone appreciates homemade jam, and this makes a nice addition to a gift basket of freshly baked breads.

4 cups diced strawberries

1 cup sugar

1/2 cup balsamic vinegar or
fresh lemon juice

Combine the berries, sugar, and vinegar in a medium saucepan and cook over medium-high heat, stirring constantly until the mixture comes to a boil. Simmer for 10 to 15 minutes, until thickened. Cool completely. Transfer to a tightly covered container and refrigerate. The jam will keep for up to 2 weeks.

MAKES 2 CUPS
Per serving (1 tablespoon): 33 cal. (2% from fat), less than 1.0 g. fat

Ginger-Tomato Relish

This relish makes a spicy dip for toasted bread rectangles, such as Scallion-Cumin Bread (see page 57), and also works well as a topping for baked potatoes.

2 cups coarsely chopped fresh
  tomatoes
1 small onion, finely chopped
3/4 cup white wine vinegar
1/2 cup sugar
3 small red chilies
2 teaspoons ground turmeric

2 teaspoons dry mustard
1 teaspoon ground cumin
1/4 cup unpeeled grated
  gingerroot
1 tablespoon salt
1 tablespoon all-purpose
  flour

Combine the tomatoes, onion, and vinegar in a medium saucepan and bring to a boil over medium heat. Simmer for 10 minutes and add the sugar, chilies, turmeric, mustard, and cumin, continuing to simmer and stirring occasionally until the mixture is reduced in volume to about 2 cups, about 20 minutes. Add the ginger, salt, and flour and continue to cook until thickened, about 10 minutes. Cool completely. Transfer from the saucepan to a tightly covered container and refrigerate. Allow the relish to mellow in flavor for 3 weeks before using. Serve at room temperature or cold.

MAKES 2 CUPS
Per serving (1 tablespoon): 22 cal. (6% from fat), less than 1.0 g. fat

Index

Almond-cherry bread, 74

Almond-honey bread, 22–23

Anise-raisin-walnut bread, 60

Apple bread, sweet, 14

Apple butter, 14

Apple preserve, 88

Apples, 44, 56–57

Applesauce, 14

Apricot glaze, 16, 17

Apricot-lemon spread, 15, 36, 68, 88–89

Apricot-pecan bread, 16–17

Baking techniques, 9–10

Banana-crunch topping, 15

Banana-granola bread, 55

Banana–whole wheat bread, 15

Beer–brown sugar bread, 46

Beet-onion preserve, 51, 89

Blueberry-spice bread, 18–19

Bran-orange bread, 37

Breakfast and brunch breads, 13–28

Brown rice and raisin bread, 35

Brown sugar, 56

Brown sugar beer bread, 46

Buckwheat-caraway bread, 47

Buckwheat-sage bread, 61

Bulgur, 68

Butternut squash bread, 48

Campfire bread, 49

Caraway-buckwheat bread, 47

Cardamom-pear bread, 80–81

Cardamom-sugar topping, 80

Carrot-nutmeg bread, 20

Cherry-almond bread, 74

Cherry–sour cream bread, 53

Chives, 66

Chocolate-cinnamon bread, 21

Chocolate-orange bread, 86

Cholesterol, 7, 11

Chutney, 44, 70, 90–91

Cinnamon-chocolate bread, 21

Cinnamon-lemon topping, 42

Citrus bread, 32

Cocoa dusting, 21

Coconut-strawberry glaze, 84

Conversion chart, 96

Cooling techniques, 10

Corn bread, 24, 66

Cracked wheat–rye bread, 68

Cranberry-maple corn bread, 24

Cumin-scallion bread, 57, 92

Currant-thyme bread, 62–63

Date–sunflower seed bread, 31

Dessert breads, 73–86

Dill-onion bread, 69

Dry ingredients, 8

Egg-free breads, 36

Eggplant jelly, 52, 60, 90

Egg whites, 11

Espresso, 21

Fat, dietary, 8, 11

Fat-free breads, 45–58

Fat substitutes, 11
Fennel bread, sweet,
    56–57
Fiber, dietary, 7, 25,
    51
Fig-pumpernickel
    skillet bread, 30
Five-grain bread, 50
Freezing techniques,
    10–11
Fruitcake bread, 54
Fruit purees, 8, 11

Garlic-scallion bread,
    65
Gingerbread, old-
    fashioned, 76
Ginger-orange bread,
    fresh, 33
Ginger-tomato relish,
    54, 92
Glazes
    apricot, 16, 17
    honey, 20, 77
    lemon, 67, 79
    orange, 20, 33,
        38–39
    strawberry-coconut,
        84
Gluten development,
    9
Gluten-free bread, 35
Granola-banana bread,
    55

Herb bread, fresh, 64
Herbs, 8, 11
Herb-tomato bread,
    72
High-fiber bread, 51,
    89

Honey, 11, 51
Honey-almond bread,
    22–23
Honey-glaze tea
    bread, 77
Honey-orange glaze,
    20
Honey-rosemary
    bread, 58

Indian pumpkin
    bread, 78
Irish soda bread,
    traditional, 36

Jalapeño corn bread,
    66
Jams, jellies, and
    preserves, 88, 89,
    90, 91

Lemon, 22
Lemon-apricot
    spread, 15, 36, 68,
    88–89
Lemon-cinnamon
    topping, 42
Lemon-pepper bread,
    67
Lemon-poppy seed
    bread, 79
Liquid ingredients, 8
Low-fat diet, 7, 8

Mango chutney, 44,
    70, 90–91
Maple-cranberry corn
    bread, 24
Maple nut–spice
    bread, 83
Maple-pumpkin
    bread, 28

Maple syrup, 11, 71
Measuring tech-
    niques, 8, 96
Mint leaves, 75
Mixing techniques,
    8–9
Mold, preventing, 10
Multigrain bread, 50

Nutmeg-carrot bread,
    20
Nutrition guidelines,
    7, 8
Nuts, 83

Oatmeal-raisin bread,
    25
Oat–whole wheat
    bread, 43
Oil, spray, 11
Onion-beet preserve,
    51, 89
Onion-dill bread, 69,
    90
Orange-bran bread, 37
Orange-chocolate
    bread, 86
Orange-ginger bread,
    33
Orange-ginger glaze,
    33
Orange glaze, 38–39
Orange-honey glaze,
    20
Oven temperature, 9
Overmixing, 9

Pans, baking, 9–10
Peach bread, fresh, 75
Pear-cardamom bread,
    80–81

Pecan-apricot bread, 16–17
Pepper, 62, 83
Pepper bread, roasted, 54–55
Pepper-lemon bread, 67
Persimmon bread/orange glaze, 38–39
Pineapple bread/ walnut topping, 40–41
Plum pudding bread, 81
Poppy-potato bread, 70, 90
Poppy seed–lemon bread, 79
Potato-poppy bread, 70, 90
Potato starch, 35
Preserves, 88, 89
Prune bread, 26–27
Prune butter, 26–27
Pudding bread, 81
Pumpernickel-fig skillet bread, 30
Pumpkin bread, 78
Pumpkin-maple bread, 28

Raisin-anise-walnut bread, 60
Raisin–brown rice bread, 35
Raisin-oatmeal bread, 25
Raisins, 37, 53
Relish, 92
Rhubarb bread, sweet, 82

Rice bread, 35, 52
Rosemary honey bread, 58
Rye–cracked wheat bread, 68

Sage-buckwheat bread, 61
Savory breads, 44, 59–72
Scallion-cumin bread, 57, 92
Scallion-garlic bread, 65
Skillet breads, 30, 49
Snack breads, 29–44
Sodium, 8
Sour cream–cherry bread, 53
Spice and sugar bread, 71
Spice-blueberry bread, 18–19
Spiced prune bread, 26–27
Spice-maple nut bread, 83
Spices, 8
Spreads, 87–92
Squash bread, 48
Storage techniques, 10–11, 22, 26
Strawberry bread, fresh, 84–85
Strawberry-coconut glaze, 84
Strawberry jam, 91
Sugar, 8
Sugar and spice bread, 71
Sunflower seed–date bread, 31

Sweet breads, 14, 56–57, 82
Sweeteners, liquid, 11
Sweet potato bread, 42, 90

Tea, 77
Thyme, 22
Thyme-currant bread, 62–63
Tomato-ginger relish, 54, 92
Tomato-herb bread, 72
Toppings, 15, 21, 40–41, 42, 80

Walnut-anise-raisin bread, 60
Walnut topping, 40–41
Wheat-free brown rice and raisin bread, 35
Wheat-rye bread, 68
Whole wheat–banana bread, 15
Whole wheat ginger-bread, 76
Whole wheat–molasses bread, 19
Whole wheat–oat bread, 43
Wild rice bread, 52

Yogurt, 79

Zest, grated, 11, 33, 79
Zesty citrus bread, 32
Zucchini bread, savory, 44

Conversion Chart
Equivalent Imperial and Metric Measurements

American cooks use standard containers, the 8-ounce cup and a tablespoon that takes exactly 16 level fillings to fill that cup level. Measuring by cup makes it very difficult to give weight equivalents, as a cup of densely packed butter will weigh considerably more than a cup of flour. The easiest way therefore to deal with cup measurements in recipes is to take the amount by volume rather than by weight. Thus the equation reads:

1 cup = 240 ml = 8 fl. oz.   ½ cup = 120 ml = 4 fl. oz.

It is possible to buy a set of American cup measures in major stores around the world.

In the States, butter is often measured in sticks. One stick is the equivalent of 8 tablespoons. One tablespoon of butter is therefore the equivalent to ½ ounce/15 grams.

SOLID MEASURES

U.S. and Imperial Measures		Metric Measures	
Ounces	Pounds	Grams	Kilos
1		28	
2		56	
3½		100	
4	¼	112	
5		140	
6		168	
8	½	225	
9		250	¼
12	¾	340	
16	1	450	
18		500	½
20	1¼	560	
24	1½	675	
27		750	¾
32	2	900	
36	2¼	1000	1

OVEN TEMPERATURE EQUIVALENTS

Fahrenheit	Celsius	Gas Mark	Description
225	110	¼	Cool
250	130	½	
275	140	1	Very Slow
300	150	2	
325	170	3	Slow
350	180	4	Moderate
375	190	5	
400	200	6	Moderately Hot
425	220	7	Fairly Hot
450	230	8	Hot
475	240	9	Very Hot
500	250	10	Extremely Hot

LIQUID MEASURES

Fluid Ounces	U.S.	Imperial	Milliliters
	1 teaspoon	1 teaspoon	5
¼	2 teaspoons	1 dessertspoon	10
½	1 tablespoon	1 tablespoon	14
1	2 tablespoons	2 tablespoons	28
2	¼ cup	4 tablespoons	56
4	½ cup		110
5		¼ pint/1 gill	140
6	¾ cup		170
8	1 cup		225
9			250, ¼ liter
10	1¼ cups	½ pint	280
15		¾ pint	420
16	2 cups		450
18	2¼ cups		500, ½ liter
20	2½ cups	1 pint	560
24	3 cups		675
25		1¼ pints	700
27	3½ cups		750
30	3¾ cups	1½ pints	840
32	4 cups or 1 quart		900
36	4½ cups		1000, 1 liter
40	5 cups	2 pints/1 quart	1120

INGREDIENT EQUIVALENTS

all-purpose flour—plain flour
coarse salt—kitchen salt
eggplant—aubergine

half and half—12% fat milk
light cream—single cream
scallion—spring onion

unbleached flour—strong, white flour
zest—rind
zucchini—courgettes or marrow